Masters of Emotional Blackmail

Understanding and Dealing with Verbal Abuse and Emotional Manipulation. How Manipulators Use Guilt, Fear, Obligation, and Other Tactics to Control People

Emory Green

CLAIM YOUR FREE GIFT

This book comes with a free bonus item.

Head straight to the last chapter to quickly claim your gift today!

TABLE OF CONTENTS

INTRODUCTION

Are they difficult, or are they toxic? I'm talking about relationships with people close and dear. No matter how close-knit relationships are, some can be quite challenging. But, some might even have transformed into a toxic relationship without you being aware of it.

However, you can determine if your relationships are healthy or toxic.

A healthy relationship requires sincerity and compassion from both ends. It helps the two involved to evolve and grow into confident and kind personalities. But what if you start feeling suffocated and controlled in a relationship? What if your needs don't matter in a relationship you rely on? Worst of all, you don't feel safe and supported to express your feelings. That makes up for a toxic relationship. Such a relationship can tear down your self-esteem to the bottom.

However, it's not easy to identify a toxic relationship. Even more so, when those relationships are dear to you. You rely on them for all your emotional support. They are the backbone of your emotional well-being. Yet, they have turned poisonous.

It's not easy to identify toxicity in relationships because the people around you, the ones you love the most, may use tactics. Tactics to manipulate you in a way that seems harmless, though they aren't. They may use them to manipulate you and get what they want. In short, they may blackmail you emotionally. But why can't you easily identify that you are being emotionally blackmailed? Simply because the blackmailers use covert techniques to manipulate you. They may make their demands seem reasonable, or make you feel selfish, or use a person of influence to intimidate you.

Ultimately, you feel pressured to give in. It becomes difficult for you to stand up for yourself, your needs, and your opinions. As a result, you endure the toxic relationship for fear of losing your loved one. The relationship and the blackmailer take over you, over your mind, intellect, and feelings. You feel frustrated, but there's nothing you can do.

Well, that's what you think and feel until now. However, there's always a ray of hope amongst the darkest of holes.

Your ray of hope is right here. It's in the secret I'll reveal in this book. A secret that helps you understand.

Understand what emotional blackmail is, what is the mindset of these blackmailers, what drives them towards emotional blackmailing, why they behave the way they do, and what shapes up the personality of these blackmailing vampires. Once you know this, I guarantee you can easily safeguard yourself from getting emotionally manipulated.

Also, if you gain an insight into the covert techniques these blackmailers use, you'll easily identify the fingerprints of emotional blackmail. How these blackmailers use words and phrases that fog your mind; how they compel you to think that they are right and you are wrong. You'll identify the methods used by blackmailing vampires to take advantage of you to get what they want.

Finally, I'll give you simple and practical steps to change this dynamic and pull yourself from the clutches of emotional blackmail. Following these tips will help you defeat emotional blackmail and regain your lost power over those who manipulate you.

How could I tell you this secret? Am I a relationship guru?

Well, ascribe it to my experience, observation, and study exploring the depths of dark psychology and covert manipulation, emotional manipulation, and blackmail. I have been exploring the tactics of motivation, persuasion, manipulation, and coercion that people use to get what they want.

My own experience led me to do so. I had been the victim of the severest form of emotional manipulation in my younger years. I have witnessed emotional abuse in a very intense form. It enslaved me with feelings of guilt for years. My heart pounded with the stigma of seeing emotional manipulation in front of me, yet staying silent about it.

Nevertheless, I got an opportunity to explore. To see and to understand what makes emotional blackmail so powerful. What is it that makes it the trickiest and prevalent form of manipulation to know and understand, especially in our close-knit relationships?

I also learned about the powerful tools, the tactics, the subtle techniques these blackmailers use to reign over our emotions. How they use our weakness against us to manipulate and get what they want.

In this book, I'm going to reveal all that I learned. If you are in a similar predicament, I don't want you to be a victim for one day longer.

Do you feel yourself being torn apart to the core, that this is being caused by one you love the most? Do you find others seizing control over your emotions? Then, you are definitely being targeted by all sorts of manipulative and coercive tactics people use to take advantage of you. But no more!

Reading this book will not only make you aware of such manipulative tactics, but also puts a sword in your hands. A sword, a powerful weapon that you can use to safeguard and protect yourself from the emotional savagery of such people.

What I'm going to reveal between these pages will empower you to define your boundaries, and will give you mental resilience to stop being taken advantage of. Not only will you feel strong, but you'll be mentally and emotionally prepared to handle such vampires and lead a peaceful life.

Understanding the techniques of those blackmailers will also help you in some self-introspection. What I mean is you'll be able to assess your own tactics in various walks of life – work, family, romantic relationships, and friendships. You can avoid the trap of being a blackmailer yourself.

Don't get me wrong when I say that. But, it's so extremely easy to fall prey to these tactics that we might even use them ourselves unknowingly. We might not only be on the receiving end of such methods, but we might also be an offender.

That's why I began tracing those methods that transform us or others from 'being human' to 'being a blackmailing vampire.' My intention in writing this book was - and still is - to pull as many people as possible from the grasp of emotional blackmail and help them lead a joyous life.

And I'm experiencing the realization of that intention every single day when I proudly bring freedom to hundreds of people by exposing these tricks.

Imagine! Imagine your life without that emotional blackmailer. No guilt, no shame, no fear, and no doubts. No more hurting or apologizing for things you didn't do. The very idea feels great! Doesn't it?

Now, turn that imagination to reality by traveling through the pages of this book that teaches you A-Z about emotional blackmail. It will remove all haze and fog from your mind and reveal the truth about your relationships. You'll be able to see your loved ones, not just for who they are, but also their intentions.

And once you see the truth, it sets you free. Free from the guilt, shame, and obligations you have been carrying for long.

So, are you ready to learn the truth of your relationship?

Before moving forward, answer this question: Is your relationship just difficult, or is it toxic? The sooner you answer, the better. Otherwise, it might be too late to fix a relationship that may blossom into something good, or too late to run from a captive relationship. The decision is yours, whether you want to be stuck with a dark relationship for your life, or take advantage of the lessons I teach in this book to build healthy relationships.

If you choose the second one, you'll come to know the genuine happiness and freedom that awaits you.

Enjoying this book so far? Remember to head to the bottom of this book for a bonus bite-sized yet valuable free resource on Conversational Hypnosis. This mini e-book is the easiest way to learn how to be a successful conversational hypnotist. Curious about the benefits it can do to your normal day to day conversations? Get your copy now! This free resource is available for a limited time only.

CHAPTER ONE:

Emotional Blackmail in Black and White

What is emotional blackmail?

By definition, emotional blackmail is an act of controlling the person with whom you have an emotional connection. This control is by using tactics that make him/her feel guilty or upset. Put simply, when any person uses your feelings (in a negative way or against you) to control your behavior or seek what he wants, it's called emotional blackmail. You can be emotionally blackmailed by your spouse, parents, children, siblings, friends, colleagues, or anyone close to you without realizing that you are being manipulated.

But why am I using the word 'emotional blackmail' and not just 'blackmail'? That's because the two are different.

Blackmail vs. Emotional Blackmail

What comes to your mind when you think of blackmail?

Probably, a movie where the villain blackmails the hero or an employee who blackmails his boss to get things in his favor.

OR

You might observe some examples of blackmail in your daily routine. A school kid threatens his classmate that he'll beat him up if the classmate complains about him. A co-worker knows some private information about his colleague and threatens to reveal it in exchange for a small fee.

To sum up, blackmail is usually associated with criminal activities, or forcefully persuading someone to give something, or follow the blackmailer's way, in return for not exposing the information that might be harmful or compromising about that person.

Yes, you understand the idea of blackmail, but what about the concept of emotional blackmail? Do you understand it as well as blackmail? Are you able to tell when it is happening to you?

I'm asking this because it's important to grasp the meaning of emotional blackmail; to understand its relevance in interpersonal relationships and society. Understanding the method is also the first step in eliminating its effectiveness, its power over you.

As previously defined, an emotional blackmailer uses your feelings against you; to control your behavior the way they want or to seek their intended objective. So the threat here is not tangible. Your feelings are used against you in emotional blackmail.

Let's get clearer with a few examples.

The husband gets caught cheating on his wife, yet he spins the circumstances, making his wife feel guilty and inadequate. He uses drama to emotionally blackmail her, and feel sorry about doubting her husband.

This situation is commonly seen in the corporate world. When one person climbs the ladder of success higher than the other person, even if they deserve it, they receive emotional blackmail for achieving so much. This may rob that person of joy, pride, and self-esteem.

One partner joins a fitness program and achieves great success with their fitness goals. The other partner may emotionally blackmail them and make them feel guilty for not spending time with them.

Strategies of emotional blackmail

An emotional blackmailer uses three main emotions against you – fear, obligation, and guilt coined into an acronym, FOG by Susan Forward, one of the USA's leading psychotherapists. For a blackmailer to be successful, he/she must know about your fears, the deep-rooted ones like fear of isolation, humiliation, or failure. The most interesting part is that these fears might be unique to you. No one else perceives them as a threat from the blackmailer except you. This gives a chance to the blackmailer to threaten you to isolate you, ridicule you in front of others, or expose your past failure if you don't succumb to his desires.

Obligation is yet another favorite tactic used by these addicts. They justify their addiction by blaming others. Instead of taking up the responsibility for their wrong behavior, they project it onto others. For example, a habitual drinker may threaten his wife by saying, "If you kick me out of the house, I'll be forced to drink more." The innocent wife believes and hopes that her husband will stop drinking if she obeys him, but it's just a trap she falls into.

Guilt-tripping is used by blackmailers to make their target feel guilty about causing some negative outcome to the blackmailer. The end result might not even be that negative, but the blackmailer presents it in such a way that the target feels pain and guilt.

The idea behind using these three emotions to control a person is that they are negative emotions, and nobody wants to experience such feelings in their life. Consequently, they give in to the demands of the blackmailer to avoid experiencing these negative feelings.

Legal definition of emotional blackmail

Emotional blackmail is a form of emotional abuse that is not legally right. That's because the blackmailer can:

- Threaten to endanger your life.
- Threaten to kill himself if you don't obey his wishes.
- Control you by using money.
- Threaten to end the relationship with you.
- Manipulate you in such a way so that you feel compassionate for him/her.
- Make you feel guilty.
- Demoralize you.
- Hurt you or make you suffer in some form.
- Deprive you of love, care, and appreciation.
- Make you feel selfish and inconsiderate.

Very tactfully and cleverly, the blackmailer makes you believe in his demands. However, the more you give in, the more the threats intensify. The only way out is to identify that you are being emotionally blackmailed. This gets easier if you know the common statements used by these emotional blackmailers to manipulate/threaten you.

Here are a few examples:

- If I ever see you with that man, I'll kill him.
- I will kill myself if you stop loving me.
- My friends and family agree with me that you're being unreasonable.
- I'm going on this vacation – with or without you.
- You can't say that you love me and still be friends with them.
- You're stopping me from spending money on myself.
- I was late for work because of you. It's your fault.
- I wouldn't be overweight if you cooked healthy food for me.
- It's your fault I'm unsuccessful in my career.

- I'll wind up in the hospital/on the street if you don't care for me.
- If you don't do this, you won't see your kids again.
- I'll make your life miserable.
- I'll destroy your family.
- You're not my son/daughter anymore.
- You'll have to feel sorry about it.
- I'll cut you out of my will.
- I'll get sick if you don't love me.
- If you can't buy me this, you're a worthless mom/dad/lover/husband.

By now, you have understood what emotional blackmail is, but it's also important to understand the mindset that drives people to use these strategies.

Why do people behave this way?

People often resort to emotional blackmail because it gives them control over other people's thoughts and feelings. They don't know how to get it another way and resort to emotional manipulation. Emotional blackmailers are very good at making their victims feel powerless and confused. They mistakenly think that by making others feel helpless and vulnerable, they'll feel powerful and good about themselves. In other words, emotional blackmail is their way of dealing with their emotional insecurities. Insecurities that might stem from an emotionally abusive childhood.

If you look into the history of these individuals, you'll often find them on the receiving end of emotional manipulation as a child. This makes it very hard for such people to know what is normal and what is not. They can't understand what a healthy relationship is and how to build one themselves. They had been bought up seeing emotional blackmail from parents, and consider that it is the right way to get things done. They find a remedy for their insecurities in repeating the cycle themselves.

Emotional blackmailers share some common personality traits:

1. Lack of empathy

It's usually not too hard for us to imagine ourselves in the other person's shoes and feel his agony, his pain, and empathize with him. But that's not so with emotional blackmailers. They can't have real empathy with others. Either they can't imagine themselves in the other person's shoes, or even if they do, it's from a position of distrust. They think that the other person is going to harm them, and thus, they are justified in manipulating them.

2. Low self-esteem

Low self-esteem? In emotional blackmailers? Are you serious?

They are capable of robbing others of their self-esteem via emotional manipulation. So how could they have low self-esteem?

I know it sounds a bit weird, but that's the truth. As explained previously, emotional blackmailers are often emotionally insecure and have low levels of self-worth. Instead of finding ways to raise their self-esteem, they believe in lowering that of others to feel good. Low self-esteem also means such people struggle to form close relationships. They might have just one close relationship and look up to it to give all the things they are missing elsewhere. This is their dependency on a relationship, and if they feel they are going to lose it, they resort to more intense emotional blackmail.

3. Tendency to blame others

Emotional blackmailers never take up the responsibility for the problems in their relationship or a failure in their careers. They always hold others responsible for their pain and suffering. Such logic makes them feel justified in threatening others to get what they want.

Chapter Summary

1. Emotional blackmail is a form of abuse where the blackmailer tries to control the other person's feelings and behavior.
2. The blackmailer uses fear, obligation, and guilt to manipulate the victim.
3. Such people lack self-esteem and empathy and blame others for their bad relationships.
4. To know if you are subject to this in your relationship, ask yourself these questions:
5. Does my partner say or do things to make me feel guilty for actions that aren't wrong?
6. Does my partner point out negative things related to my success?
7. Does my partner seek a way to bring my mood down?
8. Does my partner frequently make me feel fear, obligation, or guilt?

If you answer 'Yes' to these questions, you're definitely being emotionally blackmailed.

In the next chapter, you will learn....

- Six Progressive Steps in Emotional Blackmail.
- Common Types of Emotional Blackmailers.
- Warning Signs and Characteristics of Emotional Blackmailer.
- Blackmailer Personalities.
- Key Characteristics and Emotions of Victims.
- How to change the dynamics of blackmailer and victim transaction.

CHAPTER TWO:

The Blackmailer and the Victim Transaction

Are you feeling empowered with the knowledge gained so far? Well, you must be because now it's easy for you to pin-point the instances of emotional blackmail in your life. However, there's a common misconception people have about this situation. They tend to label every person who tries to control them as an emotional blackmailer. But common sense tells us this is not true.

If the person wants to be loved, valued, supported, or appreciated by you, he might act in a controlling way. And his wants are absolutely legitimate. Also note that demands will be made on you in any relationship, if not all the time, at least sometimes.

And it's very common to disagree with someone's demands at first, and then come to a mutual agreement, or comply with the other person's wishes even if you don't like to. But, you may do it for the love of your relationship and the other person.

The problem is not in his *'wants'* but how he goes about getting what he wants. Does he threaten you or become insensitive to your needs in doing so? Then, you can justifiably say it's a case of emotional blackmail, otherwise not.

Let's understand this with an example!

Ahana wants an iPhone from her Mom, but Mom refuses. Now, Ahana may try to get it in two ways. She may persuade her Mom by saying, "But, Sara's mom bought her an iPhone." This is clearly not an emotional blackmail. But, if she grabs a knife and threatens to kill herself if her Mom doesn't buy her an iPhone, we are in a very different place, and it's an emotional blackmail without a doubt. So the problem here is not the iPhone, but the method used to try and obtain it. It's that which helps us to analyze whether it's emotional blackmailing or not.

Moreover, if it always comes about that someone is giving in to the other's demands, then the situation has reached one of emotional blackmail.

An emotional blackmail is sometimes a transaction, perhaps even an unconscious one, between the blackmailer and the victim. The blackmailer is the *'controller'* who suffers from a dysfunctional psychological state, and who tries to control another person's emotions. The victim is the *'controlled'* who provides a reassuring reaction to this psychological state.

This transaction has 6 parts, as detailed below.

6 progressive steps in emotional blackmail

Susan Forward and Frazier identify these six stages of emotional blackmail:

Step 1: The demand

The blackmailer tells the victim (that's you) about what they want and adds an emotional threat to it. "If you don't do this, I'll kill myself."

Step 2: Resistance

Of course, you may well decline to bow down in front of the blackmailer's demands. So, initially, you resist the demand.

Step 3: Pressure

The blackmailer can't accept 'No.' So, he builds pressure upon you to give in. They don't care about how you'll feel. They are only concerned with what they want and try to grab it by hook or by crook. In consequence, they deliberately try to make you feel scared and confused by using any of their covert strategies. You begin to wonder if your initial resistance was reasonable. That's where you become weak, and they latch on to your weakness.

Step 4: A threat

A threat is the emotional blackmail itself with a statement, "If you don't do as I say, then I will…"

Step 5: Compliance

You give in to the blackmailer's threat even though you don't feel happy about it.

Step 6: Setting of a pattern

The emotional blackmail is over, but only for now. Expect a heavier demand with a much bigger threat the next time. This is because the blackmailer has identified your weak area, and he knows he can use it against you to get what he wants.

The most prevalent example showcasing these stages of emotional blackmail might even be your child. How often do you get an unreasonable demand from your son/daughter? I'm sure it's uncountable. You resist initially, may even scold your child, but ultimately give in because your child threatens you by saying, "Mom/Dad, you don't love me. Otherwise, you would have bought me this."

Result: You melt like butter and fulfill the demands without a second thought.

Can you see what your child did here? They sensed that by threatening you repeatedly with such statements, you would obey their commands and get them what they want. In short, they devise an easy way to manipulate you emotionally and have their way.

Common Emotional Blackmail Types and their Language

We can classify the emotional blackmailers into four different types:

1. Punishers

Punishers threaten to directly hurt the person they are blackmailing. They use the strategy of fear to punish you if their demands are not met. The punishment might be physical, or a financial penalty, or stopping you from seeing your friends, or withdrawing their affection, or ending their relationship with you if you don't do what they say.

A typical remark might be: "Do as I say or else I'll beat you."

2. Self-punishers

Self-punishers threaten to harm themselves as a form of blackmail and put the blame on you. They hold you responsible for doing what they do to themselves. They do so to trigger fear and guilt in you and compel you to do what they ask for.

For example, "If you don't buy me that gift, I'll kill myself."

3. Sufferers

Sufferers don't threaten you directly but will show they are sad/upset because of you. They'll blame you for their emotional state and expect you to comply with their wishes to make them feel better. Sufferers use the tactics of fear, obligation, and guilt to manipulate you.

For example, a husband says to his wife, 'You can go out with your friends if you want, but I'll feel sad and lonely if you do."

4. Tantalizers

Tantalizers also don't give direct threats, but they lure you with a promise of something better if you do what they want. Your spouse may say, "I'll buy you that necklace if you stay with me at home this weekend." However, they rarely keep their promise.

Warning signs and characteristics of an emotional blackmailer

Below are the warning signs of emotional blackmail in a relationship:

- If you frequently apologize for things you aren't doing, such as the other person's negative emotional state or outbursts.
- If your partner insists on their way and no one else's, even at the expense of other people's needs and emotions.
- It seems to be only you who is complying and making sacrifices.
- If you feel you're being threatened. If you feel intimidated into obeying the other person's demands.

As said, emotional blackmail is a vicious cycle, and as a victim, you may be inclined to apologize, plead, cry, and give in to the demands of others. But, you'll find it difficult to stand up for your needs, or address the issue directly, or communicate with the blackmailer about his inappropriate attitude. You are not able to set clear boundaries to help others know what is acceptable to you and what is not.

All this happens because you aren't aware of the characteristics of emotional blackmailers. Unless you are, you can't spot if the other person is manipulating you or not.

Any person engaging in emotional blackmail demonstrates the following characteristics:

- Insists you are crazy/unreasonable in questioning their demands.
- Tries to control what you do.

- Ignores your concerns.
- Avoids taking responsibility for his actions.
- Always blames others for their behavior.
- Gives you empty apologies.
- Uses fear, obligation, threats, and guilt to get their way.
- Not willing to compromise.
- Justifies their unreasonable behaviors and requests.
- Intimidates you until you obey their demands.
- Blames you for something you didn't do to earn your compassion.
- Threatens to harm you or themselves.

Blackmailer personalities

There's no exact prototype of emotional blackmailers, yet they demonstrate certain common characteristics.

Such people often have narcissistic tendencies or an inflated sense of self-importance. They think they are the best at everything and brag about it. Everything in their lives will center around themselves, and if this is threatened, they are prone to extreme anger, frustration, panic, or depression. Blackmailers often exhibit emotional immaturity; they're not in touch with their feelings or don't know how they exactly feel. They are likely to be people who have been on the receiving end of emotional blackmail in their early lives and have noted that it is an effective tactic.

Blackmailers have a tendency to want approval from others, often due to low self-esteem. They will create a scene out of every little issue. Although highly critical of others, they usually can't accept advice or criticism.

Some of these traits are easily visible, while some, like emotional insecurities, fear, and pain, may lie deep within their psychology.

The inner world of the blackmailer

Emotional blackmailers are cowards in a real sense. They hate to lose and can't tolerate frustration. Their frustration is connected to deep-rooted fears of loss and deprivation, and they experience it as a warning to take immediate action to avoid experiencing intolerable consequences.

Such people believe they can compensate for the frustrations of the past by changing their present. The possibilities of emotional blackmail rise significantly during crises such as separation or divorce, loss of a job, illness, and retirement, etc., any of which might undermine the blackmailer's' sense of self-worth.

It's not the crisis that makes them emotional blackmailers, rather their incapability to handle such problems. Often, you'll observe that people who are incapable of processing these issues in their life were either overprotected, or have had everything in their childhood. This gave them little opportunity to build their self-confidence and ability to handle any kind of loss. At the first hint of deprivation or loss, they either get angry or panic, and resort to blackmail to avoid experiencing that feeling.

Usually, blackmailers focus unconditionally on their desires and needs. They are least interested in other people, or how their pressure affects you. For them, each interaction with you is a make-or-break relationship scheme. If you agree to what they want, they'll stay or else withdraw from the relationship.

Blackmailers know what the relationship means to you and its importance. Therefore, they use tactics to create a potential split in the relationship. They know and realize that you won't let the relationship go. That makes you vulnerable to their manipulation.

Most blackmailers have an I-want-what-I-want-when-I-want-it attitude. And the urgency to have what they desire obscures their ability to see the consequences of their actions.

The most prominent thing to notice in a blackmailer's psyche is that they sound like it's all about you. In fact, they'll talk in a way to make you feel like it's all about you, but in reality, it's not about you at all. It's only about the blackmailer and his desires. Blackmailing flows from insecure places inside the individual doing it. Most of the time, it has to do with the blackmailer's past, rather than his present. It has to do with the blackmailer's needs, rather than with what the blackmailer says about your doings.

It takes two to blackmail

Just like it takes two to tango, it takes two for the blackmail to succeed, or even happen. The blackmailer alone can't do anything without the active participation of the victim. Unless you give the permission for the blackmail to occur, it can't happen.

Sometimes you are aware of the problem, yet you can't resist it because the blackmailer's pressure sets off a series of programmed responses in your mind, and you act out of an impulse. For example, if the blackmailer threatens to kill himself if you don't obey his commands, it doesn't leave much room for any discussion. You are immediately gripped with the fear of losing that person. You are inclined to give in, lest he takes that suicidal step. So, the blackmailer didn't even leave a space for you to think or ponder. You are bound to react impulsively.

Blackmailers are aware of your "hot" buttons. The moment you resist, the blackmailer's fear of deprivation kicks in, and they use your hot buttons to change your decision and get what they want.

So why can't you resist? Why do you play a victim to other's schemes? It's because of the characteristics that make you vulnerable.

Key characteristics and emotions of victims

Not only the blackmailers, but even victims of emotional blackmail, feel insecure, unvalued, and low about their self-worth. They doubt themselves to a damaging degree.

Victims of emotional blackmail exhibit common traits that make them vulnerable. They seek other people's approval all the time. They are afraid of anger and desire peace at any price. They often display excessive compassion and empathy. Victims of blackmail like to take the responsibility of other people's lives upon themselves. They experience high levels of self-doubt and are scared of being abandoned in any relationship they embark upon. They personalize things and generally have low self-esteem.

When you exhibit these traits repeatedly or in an extreme manner, it dooms you to the status of the 'preferred target' of an emotional blackmailer. Emotional blackmailers take cues from how you respond to daily situations or their behavior, and use them against you.

The impact of emotional blackmail

These relationships may or may not be life-threatening, but it robs the victim of his self- integrity. The victims start questioning their sense of reality. The effects of emotional blackmail on victims can be regarded as:

- Low self-esteem.
- Think poorly about themselves or believe they are of no value.
- Distorted thinking about themselves.
- Vicious cycle of blackmail and low confidence.
- The victim may even betray others to please the blackmailer.
- Feeling isolated and lonely.
- Distrust in relationships.
- Anxiety and depression.

How to change the dynamic?

After knowing the traits of the blackmailer, and yours, that makes you susceptible to emotional blackmail, it's time to spring into action. To work out how you can change this dynamic and stop being treated in this fashion.

What is necessary to stop emotional blackmail?

You must start looking at the situation in a new way. It's crucial to detach from the emotions of the blackmailer. Detachment doesn't mean becoming without feeling, but don't get distressed by their emotions. You must realize that you are being treated in a way that is not appropriate. Once you've grasped that, commit to taking care of yourself; don't allow this abusive treatment to continue. Consider the demands that are being made and how they make you uncomfortable.

Don't be tempted to give in to the pressure of the blackmailer. Set your boundaries. Take time to consider the situation from all angles, and think about the alternatives before making a decision. Have a clear vision of what you hope to achieve by changing your mindset and ways of handling the relationship.

Give due respect to your own needs first.

How to respond to emotional blackmailers?

Once you change your mindset to approach the blackmailer differently, it's time to learn the specific answers to their blackmailing statements. However, the result won't be there at the first instance. You have to practice saying these answers until they seem natural to you. Blackmailers will bombard you with visions of the extreme negative consequences of not obeying them. They'll try pressuring you to change your decision. But hold your ground.

Below are the specific ways to respond to their catastrophic statements:

1. They say: I'll land up in the hospital if you don't care for me.
   You say: That's your choice!

2. They say: You won't see your kids again.
   You say: I hope you won't do that, but I've made my decision.

3. They say: You're not my child anymore/I'll cut you off my will/I'll make you suffer/You'll be sorry.
   You say: I know you're angry/upset right now. Why don't we talk again on this subject when you're less upset?
   Threats/suffering/tears won't work anymore.

4. They say: You're being selfish.
   You say: You're entitled to your opinion.

5. They say: How could you do this to me after all that I've done for you?
   You say: I know you won't be happy about this, but it has to be this way.

6. They say: Why are you spoiling my life?
   You say: There are no villains here. We just want different things.

7. They say: Why are you acting like this?
   You say: I know you're disappointed by this, but it's not negotiable.

   Susan Forward suggests three tactics - a contract, a power statement, and a set of self-affirming phrases to stop emotional blackmail.

Contract

A contract is a list of promises you will make to yourself to stop being a victim of emotional blackmail. Take time every day to read the contract out loud to yourself.

Examples of promises:

I promise myself to no longer let fear, obligation, and guilt control my decisions.

I promise to learn and apply the strategies in this book to stop getting emotionally blackmailed.

Power statement

Create your power statement in response to that of the blackmailer, and repeat it over and over again when threatened by the manipulator. For example, "I won't do this." or "I'm not doing this." Power statements are succinct and have impact. They challenge your doubts and limiting beliefs about your capability of handling such people.

Self-affirming phrases

By giving in to the demands of the blackmailer, you may feel guilt, embarrassment, hurt, fear, shame, anxiety, anger, resentful, powerless, hopeless, etc. The only way to stop feeling these negative emotions is to start changing your thoughts. Develop some self-affirming thought-patterns to repeat whenever negative thoughts strike your mind. Ask yourself: Is the demand being made on me making me uncomfortable? Why? What part of the demand is ok and what isn't? If I comply, what will be the consequences?

Always remember SOS before responding to a demand:

STOP – take time to think about it.
OBSERVE – your reactions, thoughts, emotions, and triggers.
STRATEGIZE- analyze the demands and the potential impact of complying. Consider what you need and explore alternative options.

Since blackmailers are highly defensive, they can comment on your phrases and often escalate conflicts. Try to stay away from escalating statements, and stick with non-defensive communication such as:

- I can see that you are upset.
- I understand you are frustrated.
- I'm sorry you're angry.
- I can understand how you might see it that way.
- Let's talk about it when you feel calmer.

Handling silent blackmailers

It's easy to respond to the blackmailers who throw open threats or blackmail verbally, but what about those who sulk in silence? What can you say or do when they say nothing? This silent treatment is far more subtle than an overt attack. Sometimes, it feels nothing works with a silent blackmailer. However, if you stick to the principles of non-defensive communication, and follow these do's and don'ts, you can tackle a silent blackmailer as well.

Do's

Remember that the blackmailer you are dealing with is inadequate, powerless, and afraid that you may hurt or abandon them.

Confront them when they feel more ready to hear what you have to say. Consider writing a letter to them.

Reassure them that you'll hear their feelings without retaliating.

Be tactful and diplomatic. This assures them you won't exploit their vulnerabilities.

Say reassuring things like "I know you're angry right now, and I'll be willing to discuss this with you as soon as you're ready to talk about it," Then leave them alone. You'll only make them withdraw more if you don't.

Tell them openly that their behavior is upsetting you, but begin by expressing appreciation. For example: "Mom, I really care about you, and I think you're one of the smartest people I know, but it really bothers me when you clam up every time we disagree about something and just walk away. It's hurting our relationship, and I wonder if you would talk to me about that."

Don't be deflected from the issue you're upset about. Stay focused.

Expect to be attacked when you express a grievance. The blackmailer will experience your assertion as an attack on them.

Let them know that you know they're angry and what you can do about it.

Accept the fact that you'll have to make the first move most of the time.

Let some things slide by.

Don'ts

Expect them to make the first move towards resolving the conflict.

Plead with them to tell you what's wrong.

Keep after them for a response (which will only make them withdraw more).

Criticize, analyze, or interpret their motives, character, or inability to be direct.

Willingly accept their blame for whatever they're upset about to get them into a better mood.

Allow them to change the subject of discussion.

Get intimidated by the tension and anger in the air.

Let your frustration cause you to make threats you don't mean (e.g., "If you don't tell me what's wrong, I'll never speak to you again").

Assume that if they ultimately apologize, it will be followed by any significant change in their behavior.

Expect major personality changes, even if they recognize what they're doing and are willing to work on it.

Emotional blackmail is a painful and dysfunctional form of abuse that can tear you apart. You might feel stuck in a toxic relationship with such an abuser. But, if you hold on, and use the above tactics to respond to their threats, it will help you stop and prevent emotional blackmail in your relationships.

Chapter Summary

1. Every person who makes a demand on you in a relationship is not an emotional blackmailer.
2. It's not the demands that make a person an emotional blackmailer, rather how he goes about fulfilling those demands.
3. An emotional blackmail is a transaction between the blackmailer and the victim. The blackmailer is the '*controller*' of the victim's emotions.
4. Emotional blackmail starts with placing a demand by the blackmailer to which the victim resists. However, the resistance is short-lived as the blackmailer threatens and pressurizes the victim to comply with his wishes by using the tactics of fear, obligation, and guilt. This sets a pattern for repeated pressure on the victim.
5. Emotional blackmailers can be classified into four categories - punishers who threaten to hurt the victim, self-punishers who threaten to hurt themselves, sufferers who blame the victim for their bad emotional state, and tantalizers who lure the victim with false promises.
6. All emotional blackmailers exhibit some common characteristics - narcissistic tendency, low self-esteem, fear of

losing and abandonment, deep anger, panic, frustration, and depression, emotional immaturity, and lack of accountability.

7. Emotional blackmail can't happen unless the preferred target of the blackmailer accepts the threat and gives in.

8. Certain traits make you susceptible to emotional blackmail by others - low self-esteem, seeking approval from others, being extremely compassionate, extreme pity for others, fear of isolation, and taking on other's responsibility on your shoulders.

9. Emotional blackmail may be life-threatening or can torment the victim mentally and emotionally.

10. The only way to stop being emotionally blackmailed is to change your mindset and your approach towards the blackmailer. Setting clear boundaries, and using non-defensive communication goes a long way in handling emotional blackmail successfully.

In the next chapter, you will learn....

- The FOG - Tactics used by emotional blackmailers.
- Projection of emotional blackmail: blame, guilt, and shame.
- The emotional tools of blackmailers.

CHAPTER THREE:

Blackmailing Basic Tactics

After knowing the traits of emotional blackmailers and of your tendencies that make you susceptible to manipulation, it's time to dive deep into the tactics used by these blackmailers.

Do you know who popularized the term 'emotional blackmail'?

The leading therapists and psychologists, Susan Forward and Donna Frazier. They also introduced the concept of fear, obligation, and guilt, or the FOG. Let's know more about this FOG!

The FOG

FOG is the technique emotional blackmailers use and rely on for success. That's because their victims feel scared of them, obligated to them, or guilty of not doing what they've asked. The blackmailer knows these feelings of their victims, and soon captures their emotional triggers to allow his blackmailing to work. FOG represents the combination of three strategies that manipulators use to blackmail their victims. They can use either one, or all three, unless the victim succumbs to their demands. It stands for fear, obligation, and guilt.

Being aware of these tactics used by the emotional blackmailers will help you not to behave in a manner they want. It will help you escape manipulation and exploitation at the hands of such a person.

The three techniques used by blackmailers are:

They use your fears (F)

What's fear?

It's an emotion, a feeling that we experience when we anticipate that something bad will happen, like the fear of losing our loved ones. However, this fear also protects us from danger. Unfortunately, some people use this fear to manipulate you and make you comply with their demands. To blackmail you emotionally, the blackmailers use different kind of fears, such as:

- Fear of the unknown.
- Fear of isolation.
- Fear of making someone upset.
- Fear of confrontation.
- Fear of tricky situations.
- Fear of your physical safety.

Example: The husband knows that his wife is having an extra-marital affair with another man. He has caught them together red-handed. Yet, he can't ask his wife to stop seeing the other man because he **fears** that if he does, the wife will leave him.

They use your sense of obligation (O)

A relationship is a commitment. You are morally bound to the person with whom you are in a relationship. That's your obligation. But, when the same person uses this sense of obligation to manipulate you, to press your emotional triggers, and force you to comply with their wishes, it becomes an emotional blackmail.

For example, your partner may pressure you, and ask for what they want by reminding you of all the things they have done for you, or the sacrifices they made. This makes you duty-bound to do what they want, even if you don't like it.

They make you feel guilty (G)

If you don't comply with the blackmailer's demands, even when they use your sense of obligation, they'll use their next tactic, which is guilt-tripping. The blackmailer will make you feel guilty for not keeping up your promises as per the obligation. They'll make it seem like you deserve to be punished. For instance, you may be guilt-tripped for being happy when your partner is feeling low; you are being emotionally blackmailed.

FOG technique resides in the dark. It stems from emotions and not logical thinking on the part of the blackmailer.

However, as discussed in the last chapter, it takes two to blackmail. If you refuse to play hostage to the fear, obligation, and guilt used by this person, install personal limits, take care of yourself, and don't get blinded by your emotions, you can prevent yourself from being captivated by the blackmailer's demands.

Once he fails to captivate or manipulate you, he's less likely to try these tactics again.

What makes you hostage to the blackmailer's FOG technique?

Besides the traits that make you a victim of emotional blackmail, you fall prey to the FOG technique because of these reasons:

The need to please people - You end up giving in to the emotional blackmailer so that the other person is not angry with you. Since you are vulnerable at this point, you feel that the unjustified and unloving treatment you receive is right. You feel guilty of making the other person angry.

Wearing you down - Constant compromise in a relationship, giving in to someone's demands that don't align with your own needs and desires, can wear you down. This makes you more susceptible to emotional manipulation by FOG technique.

Fear of anger and retaliation - Most people fear other people's anger and retaliation. This fear is a powerful driving force towards becoming a victim of emotional blackmail.

Emotional manipulation by people suffering from BPD

BPD stands for borderline personality disorder. It's a mental health disorder that impacts the way the patient thinks and feels about himself and others, causing disturbance in day-to-day life. People suffering from this mental illness have self-image issues, difficulty in managing their emotions and behavior, and an intense fear of abandonment. In short, they can't tolerate being alone.

Signs and symptoms of BPD include:

- An intense fear of abandonment, so much so that the person can take extreme measures to avoid real or imagined separation.
- Having unstable intense relationships. For example, the patient may idealize someone at one moment, and then suddenly believe that the person doesn't care for them.
- Self-identity issues and seeing yourself as bad or as if you don't exist at all.
- Moments of stress-related paranoia and loss of contact with reality.
- Impulsive and risky conduct, such as gambling, reckless driving, spending sprees, binge eating, or drug abuse, or sabotaging success by suddenly quitting a good job or ending a positive relationship.
- Suicidal threats, often in response to fear of separation or rejection.
- Wide mood swings. Moods can fluctuate from intense happiness to irritability to shame or anxiety.

- Consistent feelings of emptiness.
- Inappropriate, intense anger, such as frequently losing temper, being sarcastic or bitter, or having physical fights.

The struggle with impulsivity and fear of abandonment makes people suffering from BPD resort to emotional manipulation. However, their manipulation is a way to cope with their anxieties and not a malicious plot.

How to deal with emotional manipulation by your loved one with BPD?

Though your BPD loved one has no bad intentions for you, dealing with them can create a lot of pain and emotional turmoil.

BPD author and expert, Randi Kreger has provided five steps to deal with your BPD family member or loved one. She calls her approach "Beyond the Blame System" which is an empathetic and no-nonsense way to deal with emotional manipulation by BPD sufferers.

The 5 steps of her approach include:

1. Caring for self

The first step begins with reaching out to your friends and trusted family members for support. Also, consult a qualified therapist who can guide you on how to deal with your BPD loved one tactfully. Remember not to deal with your BPD loved one when you are feeling tired, hungry, sick, or emotional. First, take care of yourself and eat right. Find ways to boost your self-esteem. Don't take your BPD loved one's behavior personally. They react out of their mental illness, and not to hurt you.

2. Know what keeps you stuck

You might have created a rescuer relationship with your BPD loved one, but it's not healthy for either of you. Perhaps actions like slamming doors, and throwing objects, have been used to control your behavior, which keeps you stuck in fear and trapped in a repetitive pattern with your BPD loved one.

Fear might control you in other ways like fear of their reactions, being afraid of conflicts, fearful of being alone, etc. Know what keeps you stuck in this unhealthy dynamic with your BPD loved one.

3. Communicate to make your point

Approaching the BPD sufferer, and trying to communicate with them, can feel frightening because the interaction was chaotic and conflicting in the past. Your attempts went in vain, and you were overwhelmed.

However, communication is the best and healthiest way of moving forward. When reaching out to the BPD sufferer, always demonstrate empathy, attention, and respect (EAR). When you approach them this way, it stands a better chance of making your loved one calm down and listen to you.

To communicate, be brief, informative, friendly, and firm. Don't be critical or sarcastic, but stick to the positives, and remain firm with your boundaries.

4. Set limits with love

This step may feel hard if you have never set boundaries with your BPD loved one, or if you've never breached them as a result of the FOG. But keep in mind, setting boundaries is essential to your mental health and the health of your relationship.

You have to communicate your boundaries with firmness as well as love. For example, if you chose to go out of the room when your loved one expresses rage, you need to clearly express that you aren't abandoning them. You need to tell them how much you love them and are leaving to help yourself, not to hurt them. You'll return only when they are calm again.

Start small while setting limits with your loved one. Be firm, but fair, and do not waver from your boundaries. Setting boundaries are commitments you make for the sake of both you and your loved one.

5. Reinforce the right behavior

Actions speak louder than words. Don't react impulsively when your BPD loved one expresses outsized negative emotions. Any reaction of this type from your side will reinforce their negative feelings, even if you only respond this way occasionally. Either walk away for a moment or address only positive contributions.

The Emotional Tools of Blackmailers

Manipulation by emotional blackmailers can include overt aggression, narcissistic abuse, and subtle forms of emotional abuse. The typical tools and tactics they use for manipulation are:

Lying

Well, nobody is 100% honest, nor a 100% liar. But, manipulators are habitual liars. They lie even when it's not necessary, not because they are afraid or guilty, but to confuse you and get what they want. Along with lying, they may put you in defensive mode with false accusations. Lying can happen through vagueness of information given, or omitting the real part and telling other things which are true.

Denial

Not realizing that you've been abused or have an addiction are not denials. Denial is to relinquish things you know, such as promises, agreements, and behavior. It also includes rationalizing excuses. For example, the manipulator may act as if you are making a big deal over a petty issue or justify their actions to make you doubt yourself or gain sympathy.

Avoidance

Manipulators avoid being confronted or take responsibility at all costs. They avoid having conversations about their behavior, which might be combined with an attack such as, "You are always nagging me." This traps you in blame, guilt, or shame.

Avoidance can also be subtle when the manipulator tactfully shifts the subject of discussion to something else. He might camouflage it with boasting, compliments, and remarks you want to hear.

Example, a husband may turn the topic of discussion by saying, "You know how much I love you" or "You are so caring and patient."

Evasiveness is another avoidance tactic that blurs the facts, confuses you, and makes you doubt yourself.

Projection - Blame, Guilt, and Shame

These are the tactics of projection. Projection is a defense mechanism used for manipulation by narcissists, BPD sufferers, and addicts. It's a defense where the manipulator accuses others of his/her own behavior. They believe in the motto, "It's not me, it's you." By putting the 'blame' on others, they put the targeted person in defensive mode; that individual now feels guilty and shameful, while the manipulator escapes as innocent.

Sometimes, even an apology may be another form of manipulation. Addicts usually blame their addiction on other people, such as a demanding boss or a spiteful spouse.

By guilt-tripping and shaming, manipulators shift the focus on to you, making you weak and, thus, getting a chance to achieve a win over you. Shaming is a step ahead of guilt-tripping to make you feel inadequate.

Shaming not only demeans your actions/behavior, but you as a person. Comparing is also a form of shaming, like parents comparing their children with siblings or playmates.

Blaming the victim also calls for guilt-tripping and shaming. For example, a wife finds evidence on her husband's phone that he is flirting with another woman. Now, the husband acts outraged because the wife has checked his phone. So he has switched the focus on to his wife, who is actually the victim. By blaming his wife for going into his phone, he has avoided a confrontation about flirting. Further, he may also lie about it or circumvent it altogether.

As a result of this response from the husband, the wife feels guilty of spying, and he will continue to flirt without worrying about the victim's emotions. The real issue of flirting remained unaddressed.

Intimidation

Intimidation is not always direct. It doesn't necessarily include direct threats to the victim each time. It can also be achieved with a look, or tone of voice, and statements like:

- I always get my way.
- I have friends in high places.
- I have contacts with many influencers.
- Do you know the repercussions of your decision?

Sometimes, the blackmailer may also resort to telling a story that evokes fear in you, such as, "She left her husband, and consequently lost her kids, her house, and everything." This is not a direct threat, but given as a warning to the victim that if he/she dares to go against them, they'll pay for the consequences just like the character in the story.

Playing the Victim

The blackmailer may persuade you to give in to their demands by playing a victim themselves. Rather than blaming you, they'll blame themselves to arouse guilt and sympathy in you. They may say, "I don't deserve to be cared for. I haven't given you much care myself, so how can I expect it from you?" This 'poor me' tactic forces you to think they are right, and you are wrong. You begin getting trapped in their manipulation and comply with what they want.

However, your compliance breeds your resentment, hurts the relationship, and encourages continued manipulation.

Once you know the emotional tools and tactics these blackmailers use to manipulate you, it gets easier to identify the instances of similar pressures and tactics in your relationships.

Now, it's time to learn the strategies for dealing with emotional blackmail.

How To Deal With Emotional Blackmail And Stop Being The Victim

The first step to deal with emotional blackmail is to know what emotional blackmail is and how you can recognize that you or someone else is being blackmailed.

Remember the following things when dealing with an emotional blackmailer:

1. Don't give in to their demands

Though the situation may sound scary if you're faced with direct physical or emotional threats, giving in to their demands will only encourage the blackmailer to repeat it. It will worsen the situation. So hold onto your ground, be firm, and refuse to comply with the blackmailer's demands. This is even more important if the threat is violence towards you or others. Remove yourself from the situation.

2. **Know that people don't blackmail the ones they love**

The most common misconception in victims about the blackmailer is that the abuser loves the victim and can abandon the relationship if he/she doesn't give in to what they want.

However, this is unlikely to be true. You must recognize that people who truly love you, who genuinely care for you, will never make demands while threatening to harm you or themselves. This will help you detach from the situation, see the reality, and have an option to refuse to follow their demands.

3. **Change the equation**

Sometimes, It won't be possible to control the blackmailer, but you can control yourself. Remove yourself from the situation for a certain period. That shows the blackmailer that he/she has no one to control. Plus, you'll be able to deal with the situation better when you're not doing it under pressure.

Whether it's you or your loved one who falls victim to an emotional blackmail, the foremost thing to know are the signs, so that the victim can be removed from the situation safely. Never take the threats of violence against the victim lightly.

How to deal with projection from blackmailers?

As discussed, projection is a defense mechanism of blackmailers, especially narcissists, BPD sufferers, and addicts. When they project, they defend themselves from unconscious impulses or traits they deny themselves or don't want to acknowledge. They believe that their emotions originate from the other person, while, in fact, it is their thoughts and feelings that are the problem. For example, they may think that the other person hates them while it's they who hate the person.

Projection is behavior that indicates low levels of emotional development or maturity.

How should you deal with projection from manipulators? Set your limits so that you don't react in anger to the projected behavior from blackmailers. Don't judge yourself based on the opinion of other people. Although it can be hard if you're a sensitive person, try not to take the projector's comments and statements personally. Try to empathize with the projector. Most importantly, don't allow anything to diminish your self-respect and belief in yourself.

Chapter Summary

1. FOG or fear, obligation, and guilt are the techniques used by emotional blackmailers for successful manipulation of their victims.
2. The need to please your loved ones, or fear of their rage and retaliation, make you susceptible to emotional blackmail by them.
3. Besides the FOG technique, emotional blackmailers use tools such as lying, denial of their promises or agreements, avoiding confrontation/conversation about their behavior, projection, intimidation, and victim playing to win over you.
4. Projection is a defense mechanism used by narcissists, BPD sufferers, and addicts where they use blame, guilt, and shame to blackmail their victims emotionally.
5. Not giving in to the demands of the blackmailers, setting your limits, and direct, firm communication with them to keep your opinion, are the best ways to deal with emotional blackmail and to stop being a victim.
6. Never hesitate to reach out and ask for support from friends, family members, and psychotherapists to deal with emotional blackmail.

In the next chapter, you will learn....

*   Effects of Emotional Blackmail on Kids.
*   Difficult parents versus toxic parents.
*   Ways to cope with blackmail in a family.

CHAPTER FOUR:

Blackmailing in the Family

The decision-making process in the family is a complex phenomenon where many factors, including emotions, play an important part. Both parents and children use emotions to influence each other and drive decisions in their favor. This is generally natural and healthy.

Healthy families make decisions on negotiation, clearly defined rules, and just authority. Though it's nearly impossible to please every family member in the decision-making process, parents attempt to listen to everyone before making the final decision. Such a discussion removes the hostage situation at home and allows everybody to express their opinions, even displeasure in the open. Thus, the issues are out in front of the family rather than one person's will imposed on the family.

Also, when rules and expectations are clear, the just authority structure is clear, the need for manipulation becomes less, and the family members develop trust in the decision made.

Using emotions becomes harmful when they are used as threats to control another's behavior or intimidate them. Parents may use threats towards children, children may use them against parents, and sometimes, even grandparents enter this cycle of emotional threats.

These emotional threats usually occur through rage, screaming, crying, whining, or complaining. They not only make the situation uncomfortable for the victim, but also forces them to do something which they don't like.

When these emotional threats take place in public spots, it becomes very embarrassing for the victim, which further adds pressure on him to yield. After several episodes of such threats, the victim is forced to give in to avoid creating a scene in public. Here, not only the psychological pressure, but the mere discomfort of that embarrassment creates pressure to give in.

Repeated emotional threats, whether from the parent or the child, creates a hostage situation within the home.

Withholding is yet another form of emotional blackmail seen within the family. The blackmailer may threaten to withhold love, attention, money, or dignity in order to have their way.

Unfortunately, many parents use emotional blackmail as a strategy for bringing up their children. They use fear, guilt, and intimidation to make their children do what they want. And the truth is that they are frequently unaware of its consequences on their children. They don't realize the effect it can have on children and the relationship they have with them.

It seems very tempting and easy to use emotional blackmail, and have children obey their commands, but the consequences are immensely damaging. Children can learn to emotionally blackmail by imitating the example set by their parents.

Why do parents resort to emotional blackmail?

Parents often resort to emotional blackmail because it gives them a way to get children to obey without protest. What they fail to understand is that control is not synonymous with education. Parents can tell the child what to do and how to do it. But, if they threaten them for not doing it immediately, they reduce the decision-making capacity in the child.

Consequently, as the child grows up, he/she will be either overly dependent or very rebellious.

Further, using emotional blackmail towards children reveals the adults' insecurity as parents. It shows they have little or no patience and can't respect a young person's way of doing things. It is also the worst way to protect yourself from your child's questions.

How does emotional blackmail affect your children?

Emotional blackmail by parents is a form of manipulation that leaves the child with no choice. They have to obey you, but probably it's short-lived. In the long run, the strategy of emotional blackmail won't work. Worst, the child may start using it against you because that's what he has picked up from you - if you can't have your way by reasonable means, threaten others to get what you want.

Additionally, emotional blackmail may fill your child's heart with resentment, which they can't explain initially but shows up as they grow older. Emotional blackmail also tarnishes the love in parent-child relationships.

Why emotional blackmail doesn't work

Sometimes, emotional blackmail by parents doesn't work because parents use threats that they don't follow up on. No parent will stop loving their child because they don't keep their room clean, so what's the point of threatening that they will?

Many psychologists have proved that these types of threats don't last long and have a very poor outcome. By using threats, you can never make your child learn and understand the real reason for keeping their room clean.

They will never learn that by having a tidy room, they can easily find their possessions. They will never learn the importance of brushing their teeth. And so on.

Most likely, when the threats seem to stop showing their effect on your child, the good habits you wanted to instill will also disappear.

In short, blackmail doesn't teach your child to solve problems or do things because it is best for them. It changes the child's behavior only for a moment, but there's no real or lasting change.

Also, if you threaten your child with a consequence, and fail to carry it out, you lose credibility in the eyes of your child. Your threats become empty.

What are the alternatives to emotional blackmail?

If you wish to tell your child to do something or how to do it, the best way of teaching is to help them or accompany them in doing the task. This is far better than shouting or giving orders from the sofa. For older children, the best teaching method is through your example. If you want them to do what you want, let them imitate your actions and attitude. Give them something positive to imitate.

Children are not robots. Only robots and machines respond to our commands the first time we ask. So you might need to repeat things more than once to make your child do them. If they delay in doing something, it isn't always laziness or a conscious act to make you angry. Children take time to learn and remember things. So let them do it at their pace.

Difficult versus Toxic parents

Difficult parents are very cautious and may cause their child to behave similarly. On the flip side, toxic parents are more inimical to their child's personality development and character formation.

You can't label a parent as toxic if:

- He/she is a bit moody.
- Stresses due to financial, relationship, or family issues.
- They're preoccupied with work.
- Physically and emotionally unavailable for their children.
- Feel resentful and bitter about being trapped in parenthood.

Such a parent is emotionally neglectful towards the child, but they're not necessarily toxic.

Here are some questions to ask yourself about your parent's behavior. If it's consistent and chronic, you might be in a toxic relationship with them.

- Do your parents overreact or create a scene over little things?
- Do they blackmail you emotionally?
- Do they place frequent or unreasonable demands?
- Do they try to control you?
- Do they criticize you or compare you with others?
- Do they listen to you with interest?
- Do they blame you often?
- Do they take responsibility for their conduct or apologize?
- Do they respect your physical and emotional boundaries?
- Do they respect your feelings and needs?
- Do they envy you?

The causes of toxic behavior from parents

The most important reason for toxic behavior from parents is basically the repetition of what they experienced themselves as a child. What they learned and imitated from their parents is now being delivered to their children in the form of abuse.

Since they didn't have enough self-awareness, knowledge, and skills to change those unproductive patterns, they continued with the same style of parenting. Also, receiving toxic abuse themselves as a child may have left them with a personality disorder or a mental health problem, which affects their ability to parent their own children correctly.

People who are parents now, if they had been traumatized in their childhood with emotional blackmail, they may well lack empathy and consideration for the needs of their child. Their child's vulnerability triggers the parent's emotional insecurities, which they can't face, and they punish the child for showing 'weakness.'

On the other spectrum of toxic parenting are those who had seemingly good childhoods, but who were 'pampered' and spoilt. They were overly-indulged and never had to wait for anything they wanted.

Such people grew up believing that their needs came first; their needs are superior to anyone else's needs, and they deserved to have power over others. They think that they should receive special attention, privileges, and rewards because they are superior to others.

Signs and symptoms of toxic parents

Toxic parents put their feelings and needs first. They are self-centered and believe themselves to be the focus of attention. They usually display erratic, unpredictable, and scary behavior. Due to these factors, they can't provide a safe and secure environment for their children.

They can't accept their child might sometimes fail because, in their eyes, this is a negative reflection upon them. Their child's failure makes them feel shameful, and they punish the child for making them feel bad. They feel jealous and envious if someone favors or appreciates their child. Due to envy, they can also turn violent towards the child's beauty or talent.

Toxic parents view their child as an 'object' on whom they can rely emotionally, physically, practically, and financially.

It's difficult, or rather impossible, for the child to please or satisfy this kind of parent. However hard they try, they are unable to please them. The child of such parents feels suppressed and oppressed. Their physical and emotional needs are neglected. Frequently, the needs of the child, even the genuine ones, feel like a burden for the toxic parent. When the child cries or craves care and attention, such a parent will belittle, ridicule, ignore, or punish the child.

Toxic parents are not interested in what their child has to say. The child's feelings and opinions are completely ignored.

Toxic parents create a severe atmosphere of tension and fear at home. Playing mind games with the child is the second nature of toxic parents. They will tell lies, give out mixed messages, to confuse and manipulate the child. They bully their child, mentally and emotionally. The child, being immature and possessing little innate gifts for reasoning, rationality, and logic is unable to question and challenge the parent's motives or behavior. The child can't dare to challenge the parent for fear of the harsh consequences.

Toxic parents exhibit passive-aggressive behavior by ignoring the child's requests and comments. Even if they promise the child something, they never keep the promise.

If you challenge the conduct of toxic parents, they may turn aggressive and violent, or give silent treatment by refusing to talk to the child.

Toxic parents showcase themselves as victims, and try to get others to believe them, and be on their side against the child.

Toxic parents are always in a 'deal' mode. They'll agree to do something for the child only if he/she agrees to their whims and fancies. The toxic parent needs to feel powerful and have control over the child's thoughts, emotions, language, and behavior. They squash the child's authentic emotional expression – even telling the child that they are wrong for having feelings.

Guilt-tripping and emotional blackmail are the favorite weapons to get their child to conform to them. Toxic parents are often highly critical and scrutinize the child's activities using sarcasm, blame and shaming comments. Toxic parents seldom respect their child's personal boundaries and will intrude upon them. They have weak boundaries themselves, and avoid making decisions or giving their child adequate guidance.

Toxic parents play double roles of a martyr and the hater. At one time, they'll say, ''How can you treat me like this? After all, I've done so much for you?'' On the other hand, they'll switch to ''I wish you'd never been born. You have ruined my life.''

Toxic parents with two or more children will play them off against one another. Both are treated differently, yet not in a beneficial manner for any one of them.

Toxic parents also may abuse their child physically and sexually.

How to cope with toxic parents?

Let's face the truth. Some individuals are so dangerous, so manipulative, and so draining, you had better stay away from them. But, what if those individuals are your parents? Is it really possible to cut off all contacts with them?

Nope! Therefore, two mental health professionals - Justin Shubert, founder of Silver Lake Psychotherapy, and Rebekah Tayebi, a clinical therapist and family coach, advise the following methods to cope with this kind of situation.

Determine if your parents are actually toxic

Look, your relationship with your parents can't be rosy at all times. There will be moments of argument where you or the parents make mistakes. Your Mom doesn't like your dress or questions you. She might say something critical which gets under your skin. She might behave the way you don't want a million times, and you feel like punching a hole in the wall.

However, all these things count for a bad equation and not toxic parents.

Toxic is when the parent's needs overtake that of the child for an extended period of time. They have extreme difficulty in regulating their emotions, or even communicating them in the right manner. Consequently, any conversations immediately flare up. Things also get very unpredictable. The psychotherapists advise you to ask yourself: Do you feel like you can breathe when around your parents? OR are you constantly suffocated in their presence because you can't be yourself and feel pressured to do what they want to please them?

Understand that typical boundaries get disrupted with toxic parents

One thing is evident from toxic family systems. The children in the family are attuned to their parents' needs. The typical parent-child relationship is inverted, and there's a lot of confusion on what boundaries to set.

For example, one parent may be in a toxic relationship with the spouse. But, they talk and argue in front of the kids rather than taking the matter behind closed doors. As a result, the kids also get involved in the parental discourse and start taking the side of one or the other parent.

Toxic parents are so absorbed in their own needs, dramas, and addictions, their children never learn how to be themselves.

Choose a go-to phrase to redirect the conversation

It's very easy for children to pick up the dysfunctional behavior of their parents and imitate them. That's why it's crucial to catch the negative patterns in the parents' behavior, and whenever possible, redirect the conversation. You can do this by modeling the type of behavior and boundaries you'd like.

For example, if your Mom's attitude becomes overbearing, you can say, "Mom, I understand it's really hard for you. But, I'm feeling quite escalated now."

So, you validate the feelings of your parents and also tell them what you experience from them. You communicate that you're feeling escalated, bowed down, or anxious, and need a break from the conversation.

Practice these responses ahead of time so that you can use them as your saving mantra to tackle the situation.

The parent may not respect your boundary, but it's much healthier for you to speak like a broken record rather than giving in to their manipulation.

Have a plan of action and a support system to rely on

Sometimes it's safer and healthier to stay with friends than with family. Maintaining a safe distance can give you a space to retreat. Have an itinerary of activities, so you have to spend the least time possible with your toxic parent.

This helps you place boundaries and decide on:

- How many days do you want to spend with them?
- Do you really want to stay with them or not?
- If you want to stay with them, do you want to bring someone along?
- How much time are you willing to spend with them in a day?
- Do you have a plan of escape if things turn worse?

Thinking about these things in advance will prevent you from falling into the old cycle of victim and regret.

Also, be clear with your support system on how you want the support. Instead of just venting out your situation to a close friend, prepare your friends for what may be coming down the line in the presence of your parents. Tell them clearly what you want from them.

Allow yourself to say "No"

Most kids who grow up in toxic parenting abandon their own needs for the sake of their parents. However, you must remember that it's not wrong to make a space for yourself and commit to it.

Remind yourself that your feelings are as valid as those of your parents, and it makes complete sense to give yourself the space you need. Take care of your feelings at that time and then get back to the family life.

Chapter Summary

1. Healthy families make decisions on negotiation, clearly defined rules, and just authority. On the other hand, when either parents or children use emotions as threats to control each other's behavior, it creates a hostage situation at home.
2. Many parents use emotional blackmail because it seems to be the easiest way to have children obey their commands without protest. Parents who resort to emotional blackmail are often emotionally insecure themselves.
3. Emotional blackmail in children reduces their decision-making capacity. They'll be either overly dependent on others or rebellious in the future.
4. Blackmail doesn't teach your child to solve problems or do things because it's in their interest. Plus, it changes the child's behavior only momentarily.
5. The best way to teach children what to do and how to do it is by accompanying them in the task or through your example.

6. Toxic parents resort to emotional blackmail because they experienced the same trauma in their childhood.

Tell-tale signs you have a toxic parent are:

- They are self-centered.
- They can't accept your failure.
- They envy you.
- You can't satisfy/please a toxic parent however hard you try.
- They neglect your needs and feelings.
- They play mind games and may call you names.
- They bully you, mentally and emotionally.
- They may be aggressive and violent to you.
- Are highly critical.
- Dealing with toxic parents begins with identifying whether they are actually toxic or not. Learn to say no to their unreasonable demands and expectations. Set your boundaries and assert them. Have friends to support you and rely on if things go awry.

In the next chapter, you will learn….

- Blackmailing in relationships.
- Seemingly innocent things that are emotional blackmail.
- Warning signs of emotional blackmail in love relationships.
- Life after toxic relationships.
- Real love versus attachment.

CHAPTER FIVE:

Blackmailing in Relationships

Seemingly innocent things that are emotional blackmail

Can you differentiate healthy behavior by your lover from toxic manipulation? Unfortunately, it's easy to mistakenly take jealousy, possessiveness, and other unhealthy actions as romance or love. Experts warn that many seemingly innocent things in love can be emotional blackmail. Sometimes, it's hard to tell.

Emotional blackmail is one of the primary ways a partner uses to control the other partner by manipulating their emotions in a way that forces them to give what they want, even outside their will.

It can take place in many forms. One such form is sarcasm. For instance, if you tell your partner or complain to them for being too critical, they'll respond by saying, "I am sorry for being such a bad person."

Instead of using this criticism in a constructive way, the blackmailing partner uses sarcasm as a manipulative response to invalidate their partner's emotions and protect their own.

According to Kelsey M. Latimer, Ph.D., founder of Hello Goodlife, emotional blackmail should never be ignored. It should be taken very seriously as an emotional abuse, and you should immediately tell the person how you feel. Also, get others involved if you feel a sense of danger.

Here are some seemingly innocent things that are actually emotional blackmail:

They want to know everything about you immediately

It's great to have someone wanting to know about you. But, it's not that great if they try to know everything right away, and push you to the point it makes you uncomfortable.

For instance, you should be cautious if they ask you about your finances too early in a relationship. You may assume that they care for money and stability, but they might not be asking for the right reasons. Especially if they push you or make you feel bad for not sharing, it's emotional blackmail.

In such a situation, it's important to set your boundaries. If you don't feel comfortable sharing, don't do it. The person who loves you will respect your boundaries.

They pinpoint your flaws

Expressing your weaknesses honestly is good, but it should never be hurtful. If your lover constantly brings up your flaws, it's an emotional blackmail. Though he/she may bring them up in seemingly harmless ways, it can trigger fear and doubt in your mind.

When you are criticized constantly, you start believing in those words. You start looking down upon yourself. You become a victim of emotional blackmail and feel stuck in a relationship because you are scared that no one else will love you for your flaws.

When the situation reaches this point, it's a clear-cut case of emotional abuse, and you shouldn't think twice about ending such a relationship.

They try to punish you after a fight

It's common to argue with your partner. But, if after the argument, your partner stays out for hours without saying where they are, it's a sign of emotional abuse. They are punishing you for the disagreement by intentionally causing you to worry or feel anxious about them.

Asking for space after the heat is fine. But, if someone intentionally does it to punish their partner, it's an emotional blackmail. When this happens the first time, approach your partner calmly, and explain your mental condition to them. If you are in a healthy relationship, your partner will make sure it doesn't happen again.

They'll test you

A healthy relationship is a balanced relationship. You don't have to go to your extremes to please your partner. For instance, if you've been longing to go on a vacation with your partner, but he insists that he'll only make it happen providing you wear dresses of his choice, that's emotional blackmail. It shows they don't welcome you in their world unless you comply with their demands.

It's a controlling behavior that makes the relationship unhealthy.

They keep an account

If your partner is an emotional blackmailer, they'll go out of their way to do things for you, but none of their actions are selfless. Indeed, they'll bring it up over and over again to remind you of the sacrifices they made for you. They'll use their good deeds to make you feel guilty and have what they want.

They turn to you for everything

It feels nice to be needed by people, but if someone starts making statements like, "You are the only one I can rely upon" or " You are the only one in my life," it should raise a red flag. No one should make you responsible for their happiness or use you as a tool to keep their problems at bay.

They want to be your everything

If you are the whole world for the emotional blackmailer, on the flip side, they expect the same from you. They want you to turn to them for everything you need. In fact, they'll do everything they can to ensure this. Though it seems harmless, it is a trap. When you have no one to turn to except them, they can easily control you.

The important thing here is to stay aware of these red flags in relationships. It's easy to regard these things as innocent and to romanticize them. But, if you find yourself in a situation of such manipulation, confront your partner and tell them how you feel. Use 'I' statements without placing blame on your partner.

Still, if you aren't able to resolve the issue, consider terminating the relationship because relationships dominated by these methods are unhealthy and emotionally exhausting.

Six warning signs of emotional blackmail in relationships

Do you know when that loving relationship transforms into an emotional blackmail? Watch out for these signs:

1. Manipulation of your decisions and choices by reacting negatively to them.
2. You are intimidated until you do what your partner wants.
3. They blame you for things that you didn't do so that you feel guilty and compelled to give in to their demands.
4. Your partner accuses you of something you didn't do.
5. They play a victim and dramatize their suffering publicly until you agree to what they want.
6. Threaten to harm you or themselves to get you to do (or not do) what they want.

People who use these techniques to control you often work in cycles. At times, you'll feel there are periods during which everything is normal. There's no guilt-tripping, or pressure to do things their way. However, such people are insecure individuals. When they start to feel out of control or uneasy about a situation, they begin to increase the pressure of manipulation on you.

If you are a victim of this kind of manipulation by your partner, seek help from a counselor right away. Besides counseling from a therapist, take these three crucial steps:

1. Set clear boundaries for yourself, and don't let the poor attitude of your partner change your mind. Giving in to them only makes things worse.
2. If your partner threatens to harm you physically, leave the location immediately, and call the authorities. Don't stay in dangerous situations simply because you fear losing your personal belongings.
3. Reach out to your friends or family or relatives for support.

However, keep in mind that many people have a certain level of emotional insecurity. And every insecure person won't turn into a monster. Sometimes your partner just needs a simple reassurance from your side. But, when reassurances don't seem enough, and you feel more and more manipulated by your partner, those are the red flags of psychological abuse. So, pay attention to these warning signs.

Are you really in love with your partner?

Love is a complicated thing. It's easy to confound attachment with love. However, here are a few differences between attachment and real love that will help you understand your relationships better.

Love is selfless; attachment is selfish

When you're in love, you focus on making your partner happy. You always think of ways to make sure your partner feels loved and fulfilled.

You don't keep a tab on who helps more, or fight over who'll wash the dishes. You neither pressure the partner nor seek to dominate the relationship.

On the flip side, attachment makes you focus on yourself, how they can make you feel happy. You become heavily dependent on your partner and even try to control them for fear of abandonment. You look up to your partner to improve your self-esteem and fill the void in you. You hold them responsible for your happiness and get frustrated if they fail to content you.

Love liberates, attachment controls

True love allows you to be yourself. If your partner loves you, they'll accept you with your strengths and weaknesses, and encourage you to be who you genuinely are. True love helps develop mutual trust and acts as a catalyst for the personal growth of the two involved. When your partner accepts you for who you are and encourages you to pursue your dreams, you'll never feel the need to control their life.

Attachment, on the other hand, fuels controlling patterns. You or your partner may stop each other from spending time with friends or manipulate each other, regardless of one's feelings.

Love is a mutual growth; attachment impedes growth

As said, love develops mutual trust, which, in turn helps in the growth of both the partners involved. It helps both of you become the best version of yourselves. In short, your partner stimulates your growth, and you do the same for them.

Attachment impedes yours as well as your partner's growth. Since you are overly dependent on them to solve your issues, and you try to control them, it impedes their growth as well. Unsurprisingly, this makes it difficult to love each other in a healthy way.

Love is everlasting; attachment is short-lived

Love is eternal. Even if you and your partner breakup, either temporarily or permanently, they'll continue to have a place in your heart, and you'll always wish them the best for their life.

On the other hand, if you were only attached to them, you'll hold resentment for them after the breakup. You'll blame them for betrayal because you considered them responsible for your happiness.

Love makes you egoless; attachment boosts ego

A loving relationship reduces your ego, fosters your growth, and makes you less selfish and more loving. Such a relationship fuels positive changes in both the partners, encourages both to open up about their weaknesses, vulnerabilities, and have communication from the heart.

Alternatively, relationships based on attachment are ego boosters. Attachment generates dependency on your partner, and you feel you can't be happy without them. You depend on your significant half to resolve your problems or help you forget them.

Dealing with emotional blackmail in relationships

If you are dealing with emotional blackmail from a loved one, you'll feel frustrated and trapped. But things can get better if you take the following steps:

Step 1: Recognize emotional blackmail

An emotional blackmailer, even if he/she is someone close to you, gains the upper hand over you because you fail to recognize their tactics. As a result, you give in to their demands and invite further manipulation from them.

Thus, it's crucial to recognize emotional blackmail before you can deal with it. Watch out for threats or punishments if you don't do what they want. The threats can be withdrawal of affection or making you feel insecure in a relationship.

Example: They may say, "If you don't want to move in with me in that house, it's absolutely fine. I knew this relationship wasn't going anywhere." Such a statement will make you feel the need to rush the relationship or risk losing them.

Notice if they threaten to hurt themselves if you don't do what they say.

Example: Your partner may say, "I know you don't love me or care for me; otherwise, you won't refuse to give me money. I am such a bad husband. I don't deserve to live anymore."

Observe when your loved one tries to make you feel guilty for no reason. The blackmailer may try to accuse you of hurting them, even though you haven't done anything. Beware if this guilt drives you to do things for them, it may be an emotional blackmail.

Example: Statements like, "You never do what I want." Or, "My friends say you neglect me" may make you feel guilty.

Take note of the times when they try to make you feel a sense of duty. Being in a relationship, you have a responsibility towards your family, friends, and your partner. However, if your loved one tries to make you accept a sense of duty when you don't, they are trying to manipulate you. Doing it this way, the blackmailer tries to convince you to take on a role or responsibility that isn't yours.

Example: Your neighbor may ask you to babysit her kids for free.

Beware of their blaming strategy. Blaming is a form of emotional manipulation to get you to do what they want. They'll accuse you of things you haven't done.

Example: Your wife lost her job due to her careless attitude. However, she might blame you by saying, "I lost my job because you never bought me better work clothes."

Realize when your loved one puts their needs before yours. This shows that they care only about themselves, and, therefore, they expect you to tend to their needs.

Example: If your partner asks you to leave your work to listen to his issues, but cuts off when you wish to vent about your situation.

Step 2: Set your boundaries

Don't give them what they want

Saying 'Yes' to the demands of the manipulator will reinforce their conduct. Even if their threat seems overbearing, hold your ground, and stay firm. If they continue pushing you, step away to take a few moments for yourself. Ask a friend or a relative for support.

Be empathetic towards their situation but don't give in to their demands. If they threaten to harm you, call the emergency services. If they threaten to harm themselves, call for help and stay with them. Enquire about what they are feeling at the moment.

Don't take their comments personally. Ignore certain things they say to get attention, by continuing your side of the conversation as if they didn't say anything.

Tell them to clarify their intentions

This will help you determine any inappropriate attitudes or actions without blaming or accusing them. It also forces them to state what they want clearly and allows you to address them without worrying about their emotional threats.

Clearly state what you'll accept and what you won't

Setting your boundaries and telling others about it gives them the guidelines about how to behave around you. Tell them straightforwardly that you won't accept any manipulative tactics. Instead, if they want something, they should tell you clearly.

You could say, "I won't listen to you if you scream and shout at me. I'll leave the room. However, I am ready to listen if you speak in a soft, calm tone."

Take their threats of violence seriously

It's important you take their threats of violence seriously and call for help, whether they threaten to harm you or themselves. If they threaten to harm you, remove yourself from the situation immediately and, if need be, call the police.

Don't hold yourself responsible for their feelings and actions

Individuals like this blame you to make you feel guilty, and they act as if you are responsible for their feelings and actions. The truth is they are responsible for their feelings, while you are responsible for yours.

For instance, they may try to blame you for their bad mood and expect you to fix it. Though there's nothing wrong in making someone cheer up, they shouldn't manipulate you for that. Your responsibility shouldn't revolve around that only. You could empathize with them and say, "I am sorry you had a bad day. I can't change that, but I would like to enjoy a nice evening with you."

Follow through if they overstep your boundaries

While setting your boundaries, it's also essential to decide the consequences if anyone breaks them. Emotional blackmailers will try testing your rules. So you have to stand firm and do what you promised to do if they broke your rules.

If you said that you'd call the police if they threatened you violently, then follow through. Doing so makes them realize that your rules are for real, and they'll respect them. Otherwise, neither you nor your boundaries will receive recognition, and you'll invite more manipulation from them.

Take a break from the person if the problem is grave

If your loved one continues to pressure you, it will take a toll on your emotional health. So it's best to protect yourself and spend some time away from them. That will also make them realize that you won't tolerate manipulative or bad behavior.

Step 3: Confront the person

Call them out when they blame you

Tell them that you won't take responsibility for their actions. Ask them to accept the blame for their actions and encourage them to solve their problems.

You can say, "It's not my fault that you forgot your phone this morning. I am sorry you had to stay without your phone in the office today, but you must accept responsibility for your actions."

Express your feelings about their conduct

Since emotional blackmailers are more focused on their feelings, they may fail to realize that they are hurting you. So it's your duty to tell them how their actions affect you, that you are the victim, not them.

Adopt a non-defensive way of communication

If you blame or accuse them in reciprocation, they'll turn defensive and manipulate you more. This makes it difficult to resolve the issue. So adopt a non-defensive way to communicate with them. Such as:

- Don't deny their complaints immediately.
- Take turns to speak.
- Don't accuse them of anything.
- Don't point out their actions to justify yours.

Use "I" statements

When pointing out the way they behave, use "I" statements to keep the focus on how you feel rather than blaming them. This reduces their risk of becoming defensive and pulling away from the conversation.

Ask them to help you solve the problem

This makes them see that you are their friend, not an enemy, and they may transition to your side. It makes them feel safe that you aren't attacking them.

You can say, "I know we've had a tough time communicating with each other. I really want to have a good relationship with you. Do you think we can work together to solve this?"

Step 4: Coping with a manipulative loved one

Recognize your emotional triggers

Your loved ones, especially those closest to you, have a special ability to manipulate you because they know you in and out. They know the emotional triggers they can use to get under your skin. These triggers could be:

- Love can be used to soften you.
- Anger and apathy.
- Criticism to make you feel guilty you aren't doing enough for them.
- Their suffering.
- Helplessness.
- Explosiveness to make you feel scared of them.

Listen to their feelings without changing your mind

Sometimes, your loved one may be in actual distress. It helps to talk it out with them and listen to what they feel. However, you can't necessarily give them what they want. Otherwise, you'll invite manipulation.

Step away from their tantrums

If their actions are out of control, such as throwing a tantrum or crying endlessly, take a break from the situation. They feel that by being so dramatic, they can make you feel bad and manipulate you. It's important to realize at this moment that you are not causing them to behave this way. They are doing it themselves.

Give them the benefit of the doubt when they behave nicely

Unfortunately, emotional blackmail may turn you skeptical towards your loved one, and you begin to doubt their intentions, even when they are not manipulative. Accusing them of manipulation when they aren't doing this, can harm your relationship.

Model good behavior

You can accidentally teach your loved one to blackmail emotionally by doing the same with them, especially children. Instead, set an example for them by behaving the way you would like them to. Have a healthy communication with them, be responsible for your actions, and follow the family rules.

For example, don't try to control your child by saying, "You spoiled my mood. You've made me sad." Don't break their possessions if you feel angry.

Life after toxic relationships

Finally, if all the methods to cope with a toxic relationship have failed, you have to end that relationship. It's natural to feel bowed down after that, and spend a few days grieving. However, some people experience what is called post-traumatic relationship syndrome. It's a mental health syndrome that occurs after experiencing trauma in an intimate relationship. These feelings can prevent you from finding a healthier relationship in the future.

Signs of post-traumatic relationship syndrome

1. Afraid of making another commitment

It's OK, and even healthy, to take time, after a breakup from a bad relationship, before you commit to a new relationship. If you wish to seek another relationship but can't make yourself do it, you may still be under the trauma of the last relationship. You are in self-doubt and experiencing low self-worth. In such a case, seek support from friends or even a counselor to figure out the ways to move past the trauma and learn to trust again.

2. Feeling unworthy or unconfident

If you feel downtrodden and worthless after a break-up, it's a sign of trauma. Such thoughts are a side-effect of harsh words from your ex who could have manipulated you to the extreme and eroded your self-esteem. Though tough to shake, it's possible to get rid of such thoughts with the help of a therapist.

3. Feeling guilty

Once the relationship ends, you'll heave a sigh of relief. But after a few days, you may be surrounded by feelings of guilt and self-doubt. The toxic relationship created such a dependency in you, it's common to wonder, "Did I do the right thing?" or "Was it really my fault?" At this stage, many people get back with their ex to make this discomfort go away. That may be fine in some cases, but rekindling with a toxic ex? Give yourself plenty of time to think over what you went through in that relationship, and whether you genuinely want to get back with them.

4. Feeling isolated and lonely

Yet another feeling that envelops you after the break-up is the intense feeling of loneliness. There's a general sense of wasted time, days, months, and years of life. It can put you in a very vulnerable state. It can also lead to rebound relationships as you struggle to free yourself from these negative emotions.

5. Engaging in another unhealthy relationship

If you don't give yourself time to recover from the toxic relationship, or treat your trauma, or learn about the traits of a healthy relationship, you may immediately fall into another relationship that's equally bad.

6. Difficulty in letting it go

It's common to feel low after a break-up, but all the more difficult to move on from a toxic one. You may focus on things your ex said, try to replay those scenes, or wonder how they could have been different.

It's possible to shift your attention from your ex, focus on the self, and fill your brain with healthier, positive thoughts. Take help from friends or a trained therapist who can help you address the issues you have in letting it go.

7. Having intrusive thoughts

It's OK if you get thoughts about your ex or what went wrong once in a while. But check if you are getting obsessed with such thoughts. This can make you doubt your choice in relationships, and you'll find it hard to trust the process of relationship building. It will be hard to trust your instincts about others. All this leads to distraction, acting impulsively, disturbed sleep, or constant crying and irritability. Consulting a therapist will be the right choice to help you move on.

8. Feeling distrust in new relationships

When you go into a new relationship without healing yourself of the past wounds, it's common to expect those bad things to happen all over again. After exiting a toxic relationship, you can often find yourself reacting to friends, family, or new relationships with suspicion.

Being aware of this tendency is the first step in recovery. You must be aware if you are sensing something negative in new relationships, but also if you're labeling a simple mistake by your new partner as something harmful. This can tar your new relationship.

Talk to your therapist or loved one to help you overcome the marks of trauma and deal with these trust issues.

9. Feeling insecure

The trauma from the past toxic relationship can also make you insecure, and you may find yourself frequently apologizing to the new partner. When you've been in a toxic relationship, you develop coping patterns to keep arguments to the minimum. Most of these coping patterns consist of apologies and saying sorry for your thoughts, feelings, and actions. This conditions your mind to believe that, by apologizing, you can control your partner's reaction. And you continue the same with the new partner to protect yourself from the hurt previously experienced.

10. Feelings of anxiety

Look out for any signs of stress you may have, especially those to do with your relationships. Post-traumatic relationship syndrome mainly stems from the fear and mistrust in relationships.

There could be many other causes of anxiety. So don't jump to any conclusion that you were in a toxic relationship or were traumatized simply due to this feeling of anxiety. If it's in line with what you experienced in the past, it could probably be the cause. Seek treatment from the therapist if necessary.

11. Having flashbacks and nightmares

It's possible to have flashbacks to past moments or wake up in a cold sweat from a bad dream after leaving the toxic relationship. You can experience bouts of anger and sadness, or waves of self-doubt, and take too much of the responsibility for what happened.

Since all this is not healthy for you, it's important to seek help and support as soon as possible. This will help you move past the trauma and create healthier relationships in the future.

How to maintain your grace after a bad break-up?

The most serious consequence of breaking up from a toxic relationship is that you can lose all your calmness and try to hurt your ex the way they have hurt you. However, you can stop all this from happening to you; handle your break-up with grace by following these steps.

Remember not to be in the attacking mode after the breakup. It's natural to feel a desire to get back at someone, but this only sets a cycle of spiteful interactions from which it'll be hard to recover. Instead, acknowledge your hurt and take time to recover from it.

Admit your negative feelings after the break-up and deal with them healthily rather than denying them behind a false mask of strength.

Never use your vulnerability in this period to emotionally blackmail your ex. That will only invite guilt and resentment. You'll have to take responsibility to recover and regain your emotional strength.

Distance yourself from your ex to take time to recover. Avoid their favorite places, mutually favorite places, and meet your common friends separately. Brooding over your relationship will only aggravate your pain.

Respect your ex's secrets and don't reveal them to your friends to take revenge for what they did. Remember, your secrets are in your ex-partner's possession, and they can do the same thing with you.

Don't announce your breakup and negative feelings on social media. Keep away from posting those sad songs, and cryptic status updates, on social media. Don't let your inner state tarnish your social media image.

You might feel guilty and resentful after the breakup. However, don't let this resentment influence your decisions in the present and for the future. In fact, shift your focus from resentment to healing yourself from those wounds.

Find a friend or a support system where you can express your emotions - anger, rage, sadness, vulnerability, etc. Also, find an activity to convert this rage into something positive. It could be something artistic or perhaps going to the gym.

Avoid the outbound gossip about your break-up in your social group. Don't reveal the details to everyone. Keep things confidential by revealing only to a small group of trusted friends.

After the break-up, it's natural for your ex to behave like an ass, refusing to return your stuff, badmouthing you to friends, or other obnoxious behavior. Counteract his behavior with calmness, kindness, and dignity.

Chapter Summary

1. Jealousy, possessiveness, and other unhealthy feelings are often mistakenly taken as romance or love.
2. There are certain things in a loving relationship that seem innocent but might be emotional blackmail. If they want to know everything about you right away, if they point out your flaws that don't exist, if they try to punish you after an argument, if they test you or keep a score of all the good deeds they've done for you, or turn to you for everything, or want to be your everything.

3. You can tell if you are in a loving relationship with your partner or merely attached. When you are in love, you'll reduce your ego, foster each other's growth, be loving, and not self-centered.

4. Alternatively, if the relationship is based on attachment, it will be dominated by ego. You'll focus on how your partner can make you happy, and become overly dependent on them to solve your life issues.

5. To deal with emotional blackmail in relationships, be aware of the warning signs, set your boundaries, be firm with them, and if the situation gets out of control, break-up from that toxic relationship.

6. It's natural to feel bowed down after ending a relationship with a loved one. Accept the help of a trained therapist to overcome the negative feelings, vulnerabilities, rage, and fear that envelops you in that time period.

In the next chapter, you will learn….

- What is codependency?
- Signs you are in a codependent relationship.
- The link with Sociopaths, Psychopaths, and Narcissists.
- Codependent parents.

CHAPTER SIX:

Codependency

What is codependency?

Codependency is a state of depending on other people for your emotional gratification, and for the carrying out of both essential and inconsequential daily and psychological functions.

In short, codependent people are needy, demanding, and submissive. They always fear others abandoning them. Therefore, they cling to them and behave immaturely. Codependents can go to any extremes to safeguard their relationship with their companion. They can even let themselves be abused or maltreated., but will remain committed to the relationship.

Thus, by accepting the role of victims, codependents control their abusers and manipulate them.

Types of codependency

There are 4 types of codependent behavior based on the root cause of their codependency:

Codependency to fend off fear of abandonment

These people can't bear their friends, spouse, or family members to desert them or attain true autonomy and independence. As a result, they are clingy, prone to panic, smothering, and display self-annihilating submissiveness.

Codependency to cope with the fear of losing control

Such people feign neediness and helplessness, and get people to cater to their needs, wishes, and requirements. They are 'drama queens,' refuse to mature emotionally, and force their loved ones to treat them as emotionally/physically invalid individuals. These types of codependents use emotional blackmail, and even threats to secure the presence and compliance of their loved ones.

Vicarious codependents

Vicarious codependents live through others. They sacrifice their own needs, opinions, and requirements for the sake of others, only to get their approval and keep them in their life forever. Also known as inverted narcissists, these people crave to be in a relationship with a narcissist irrespective of how much they abuse them. They actively seek relationships with narcissists and ONLY narcissists. They feel empty and unhappy in a relationship with any other kind of person.

Signs you are in a codependent relationship

It's sometimes hard to know if you are in a codependent situation. However, if you find yourself in a relationship, and you rely exclusively on it for feeling better or happy, you are likely to be in a codependent relationship. The feelings you associate with such a relationship are actually of infatuation rather than love. These feelings are more strongly experienced than the normal feelings associated with seeing or hearing from your partner. It's a state of euphoria.

A codependent relationship is like an addiction. It takes complete hold of you long before you realize it. Consider the following to know if you are in a codependent relationship:

- Do you often apologize or make excuses for your partner's attitude and actions in public or in front of friends and relatives?
- Do you fear to speak about your opinions or concerns in front of your partner?
- Does being around your partner give you feelings of low self-worth?
- Does your partner treat you with disrespect?
- Is your partner jealous of your accomplishments? Does he/she try to demoralize you, or criticize, or make you feel bad about yourself?
- Do you feel like your partner is too dependent on you and can't function without you?
- Does your partner threaten to harm themselves if you try to leave the relationship?
- Is sexual attention interpreted as love or affection by you?

If you answered 'Yes' to any one or all of these questions, you might be in a codependent relationship. However, codependency is often a two-way street. Not only your partner, but also *you* may be the perpetrator of codependent habits.

When you are codependent, you'll suffer from low self-esteem, and exhibit passive-aggressive or controlling psychological states. For instance, rather than telling your partner how you feel about a particular thing, you'll react by ignoring them or lashing out at them. You may also overreact on petty issues or use abusive language to control others.

8 warning signs you're in a codependent relationship

1. You start filling in the gaps

In a codependent relationship, one person starts taking complete responsibility for keeping in touch. If one partner starts pulling back on how much time, energy, and care they give, the other partner instinctively starts filling the gap by working harder to stay bonded.

2. Desire to 'fix' your partner

Codependent personalities are people-pleasers; they thrive on helping others or even think of 'fixing' them.

3. You lose your boundaries

Codependent individuals are over-givers. They continuously feel the need to give to others even at the expense of their own needs. They feel overly responsible for others or care too much for them. However, in the compulsion to give, they often neglect their boundaries and even let others intrude on them.

4. You don't have an independent life

When you become so dependent on someone that you lose who you actually are or the essence that makes you unique, you are in the trap of a codependent relationship.

5. You lose contacts with friends and family

When you start losing touch with your loved ones or those who are important to you, it's a sign of something grave. Your primary focus is on your partner, but it shouldn't be to the point where you're becoming isolated from the people previously important to you. You should be aware of this, and consider it seriously; otherwise, you'll become more and more dependent on your partner. Sometimes, if you decide, you aren't meant for each other, you'll look around for old friends but won't find any.

6. You always have to ask for approval

If you feel you have to get the permission of your partner for daily basic things or you can't make a decision without them, you are very possibly in a codependent relationship. If you had loads of confidence when you entered the relationship, but over time, you began to doubt yourself and became indecisive, you could be in an abusive codependent relationship.

7. Your partner has unhealthy habits

One of the early signs of a codependent relationship is when one person repeatedly engages in unhealthy habits like heavy drinking or binge eating. The other person either joins them or encourages it for his or her own reasons.

Example: Sara knew her boyfriend was pre-diabetic and should stop eating sweets. Yet, she never accepted this because of the good feelings she got from her boyfriend's appreciation of her recipes. So, despite knowing the truth, Sara kept promoting her boyfriend's unhealthy eating so that she could feel good.

8. You always chase reassurance

Ask yourself these questions:

- Do you or your partner always worry that the other person will break off the relationship?
- Does either of you need constant assurance that you are loved?
- Does either of you create tests to get the other person's attention?
- Does either of you flirt with people outside the relationship to evoke jealousy in one another, so that, if one threatens to leave, they can be begged to stay?
- Do you avoid direct conversations about the state of your relationship?
- Do you have difficulty being alone?
- Is your relationship extremely tense, and both of you enjoy the drama of breakups and reunions?

If you answered 'yes' to any of these questions, you are probably in a codependent relationship.

If you are in a healthy relationship, you'll celebrate each other's accomplishments, show respect to each other even if your opinions differ, and feel comfortable expressing your thoughts with each other. You'll feel loved and appreciated, happy in each other's company in public, be respectful of each other's privacy, and trusting towards one another.

On the opposite side, if you are in a codependent relationship, you'll be jealous of their accomplishments, fear speaking out your feelings to the partner, withhold your affection, spy on them, and feel resentful and suspicious about them.

Codependency shares some common symptoms of addiction like feelings of denial, low self-esteem, inability to adhere to or set boundaries, dysfunctional communication, and controlling attitudes.

Understanding the codependency bond with sociopaths, psychopaths, and narcissists

Reading from above, it may almost sound like codependency is a disease. However, it's an emotional and behavioral condition that is stored in your subconscious mind. It affects your ability to have a healthy relationship with others.

Psychotherapists call codependency a 'relationship addiction.' And, just like an addiction, a codependent relationship is based on insecurity, denial, control, and manipulation.

Someone who is a relationship addict may threaten to harm themselves if their partner thinks of ending the relationship with them, or they'll use other forms of emotional blackmail to control their partner. The person trapped in a codependent relationship, or the one who plays a passive role, frequently ends up putting more and more effort into pleasing their partner and sidelines their own needs.

To understand the bond between codependency and sociopaths, psychopaths, and narcissists, it's important to understand these three types of personalities.

Who is a sociopath?

The term 'sociopath' is used to describe a person who has an antisocial personality disorder. Such people can't understand another's feelings. They'll break rules, or act out of impulse, without feeling guilty for their actions. Sociopaths also use 'mind games' to control friends, family, colleagues, and their partners. To label someone as a sociopath, their psychology must show at least three out of these seven traits:

1. No respect for social norms or laws.
2. Telling lies, deceiving others, using false identities, and using others for personal gain.
3. Behave without thinking of consequences.
4. Shows aggressive behavior and gets into fights with others at every occasion.
5. Doesn't consider their safety or that of others.
6. They don't follow up on personal or professional responsibilities.
7. Don't feel guilty for hurting or mistreating others.

Who is a psychopath?

The term 'psychopath' also refers to antisocial personality disorder. Therefore, it's frequently used interchangeably with sociopaths. Both the descriptions are used under an umbrella term of Antisocial Personality Disorder (ASPD).

The common signs of a psychopathic mental state include:

1. Socially irresponsible conduct.
2. No interest in the rights of others.
3. Inability to differentiate between right and wrong.
4. Difficulty in empathizing with others.
5. Tendency to lie.
6. Manipulating and hurting others.
7. Recurring problems with social laws.
8. Disregard towards safety and responsibility.

What is narcissistic personality disorder?

Narcissistic personality disorder is used to describe an individual who is excessively full of themselves. It can be mistakenly perceived as self-love, but it's not a healthy sort of self-love. Narcissistic personalities need constant admiration and consider themselves to be better than anyone else.

They're in love with this inflated or exaggerated self-image that often masks deep feelings of insecurity. They exhibit self-centered behavior, lack of empathy and consideration for others, and excessive need for admiration. This thinking and conduct surfaces in every walk of life: work, friends, family, and love relationships.

Signs and symptoms of narcissistic personality disorder

1. Grandiose sense of self-importance.
2. They believe they're better than everyone else and should be recognized as such, even when they haven't done anything to earn it.
3. They exaggerate or lie about their achievements and talents.
4. Living in a dream world with self-glorifying fantasies of unlimited power, success, brilliance, and attractiveness characterize narcissistic personalities.
5. Narcissists need constant admiration to feed their egos. So they surround themselves with people who will feed their obsessive craving.
6. They expect favors from others as their due, their birthright.
7. They expect others to always comply with their whims and fancies.
8. If you fail to admire or praise them, they'll consider it as a betrayal
9. They view people in their lives as objects to serve their needs and can't empathize with anyone.

10. They feel threatened by people who are confident, popular, or who challenge them in any way.
11. They use bullying, insults, name-calling, and guilt to make others comply with their needs.

Despite all these shortcomings, narcissists often have a charming and magnetic personality. It's very easy for them to attract others by creating a fantastical, flattering self-image. Their apparent confidence and lofty dreams are often seductive enough to mesmerize anyone. Yet, it's wise to be cautious around such people.

If you think narcissistic personas can fulfill your longing to feel more important, more alive, you are very likely mistaken. Generally, it's only a fantasy with 0% reality.

How is codependency related to sociopaths, psychopaths, and narcissistic personalities?

Codependents lack a healthy relationship with themselves. They are prone to put others before themselves. They are so dependent on others for emotional gratification that they sideline their own needs for the sake of keeping the relationship.

Thus, codependent individuals are vulnerable targets for sociopathic, psychopathic, and narcissistic personalities. Since these personalities regard themselves as above everyone else, they use and exploit the codependent individuals without any guilt or remorse.

Codependents and sociopaths/psychopaths/narcissists find each other like the two pieces of a puzzle. When one is extremely giving, and the other is extremely demanding, they make the perfect duo of an abuser and the victim.

Codependent parents

Codependency doesn't necessarily exist between a boyfriend and girlfriend or a husband and wife. It can be between a parent and a child as well. The caregiver nature of parent-child relationships often makes it difficult to detect codependency.

However, here are a few signs that could indicate codependent parents:

Victim mentality in parents

A codependent parent believes that other people, particularly their children, are responsible for the wrongs committed to them in life, and therefore, they expect them to pay the compensation. Thus, they often exhibit guilt-tripping tactics to harness sympathy from their children. Instead of dealing with their life issues and traumas, and seeking a positive solution through counseling or therapy, the codependent parent latches onto the child and asks for compensation.

For instance, a father who could not achieve higher success in sports may demand that his son excel in sports and make up for his loss. If the child denies him, he'll use manipulation and guilt to make them comply.

The codependent parent is never wrong

Two people in a relationship can't be right all of the time. But in a codependent parent-child relationship, the parent is always right; at least the parent thinks so. Even when the child grows up to be an adult, the parent refuses to approach a discussion with openness and thereby avoids the possibility of being wrong. Instead, the parent will try to impose his/her view on the adult child and "correct" the child.

Such a parent never listens to the child's feelings and problems; they never learn about their child's personality, fearing it as a challenge to their authority.

If it's revealed that the codependent parent is wrong, they'll never apologize, or, if they do, they do it insincerely. A codependent parent wants absolute dominance over the child, and any weakness on their part will threaten this dominancy.

The codependent parent is extremely emotional

Crying, yelling, and silent treatment are the favorite weapons of a codependent parent. When they feel they're losing control in a situation or can't have the upper hand in an argument, they resort to crying, screaming, and other forms of intimidation to turn things in their favor.

If you point out their manipulative ways, they'll accuse you of being callous or insensitive. Further, if the child cries or expresses his hurt, the codependent parent gets angrier, often claiming the child's distress is insincere and manipulative.

The codependent parent is a poor listener

The codependent parent doesn't have a hearing disorder; nevertheless, they are poor listeners because they never listen/consider anyone else's opinion. Talking to a codependent parent may feel like 'talking to a brick wall.'

If the argument or the discussion is valid, even if you present irrefutable facts, the codependent parent will deny them and won't be moved in their position. They'll change the topic of discussion from the actual point being made.

The codependent parent imitates your words and phrases

If a child expresses his/her feelings to a codependent parent, the adult will mimic them. For instance, if the child says that the parent is upsetting them, the parent will reciprocate by saying, "You're hurting my feelings."

Whatever concern the child expresses, the codependent parent will turn it and adopt it as their own. If this is pointed out, the parent will ignore it, get angry, or act bewildered and confused.

The Codependent parent has mood swings

The codependent parent rapidly shifts from one mood to another to avoid responsibility and guilt. This especially happens when their manipulation tactics have succeeded in garnering the child's compliance.

For example, a mother rings her daughter in college and screams at her for not phoning often enough. Her manipulative tactics may eventually get the daughter to obey her and call more often. Once the mother achieves this, to maintain her victory and her role as a victim, she may say, "No, it's OK. You need not call me often. You'll only be doing it because I have asked you to do so."

In this case, the daughter will be persuaded to not only call her more but also reassure her that she's doing it out of her own free will.

Codependent parents wants to control at all costs

Control is the end goal all codependent parents desire. They expect love and devotion from their children to make up for the lack in other relationships. Often, the codependent parent will seek to gain from their child the love and attention they didn't receive from their parents.

The codependent parent seeks to gain control even over the adult child. If it becomes clear that they won't succeed, a meltdown often ensues. When the adult child refuses to give the parent what they want, they'll attempt to control with guilt by appearing frail, playing a victim, or using aggressive strategies.

The codependent parent uses subtle manipulation

Examples of subtle manipulation include silent treatment, passive-aggressive comments, denial of wrongdoing, and projection. The codependent parent uses all these forms of manipulation to leave their child confused as to "Who's the real bad guy?"

Codependent parents are often oblivious to their manipulations. They believe they are doing it in their child's best interest. When you call them out on their manipulation, they get genuinely and deeply hurt and bewildered.

A codependent parent usually manipulates, not because they *want to*, but because they *have to*. That's because they don't know any other way to communicate with their adult child. So, they'll manipulate with finances, emotions, guilt, or any conceivable method to maintain their codependent relationship.

What should you do if you have a codependent parent?

The right way to deal with such parents depends upon the severity of the situation. In some cases, you may have to end the relationship completely. In others, you have to set your rules, carefully impose them, and perhaps look for a family therapist to help you maintain a healthy relationship with them.

Chapter Summary

1. Codependency is the mental and emotional dependency on others. Also known as 'relationship addiction,' it makes you demanding, submissive, and live in fear of abandonment by your loved one.

2. Codependents are vulnerable targets or victims of emotional manipulation because they allow abusers to control them for fear the abuser might leave the relationship.

3. If you rely exclusively on a particular relationship, whether parents, spouse, friend, or lover, to feel better and happy, you are possibly in a codependent relationship.

4. Two partners in a codependent relationship are often jealous of each other's accomplishments, are afraid of speaking about their feelings to each other, or will spy on each other out of suspicion.

5. A codependent relationship is based on insecurity, denial, control, and manipulation.

6. Sociopaths or psychopaths are the terms used for people suffering from Antisocial Personality Disorder. Such people have no concern for social norms and will exhibit socially irresponsible behavior without thinking about the consequences or considering other people's feelings and safety.

7. Narcissists have an inflated sense of ego and believe themselves to be better than everyone else. They crave praise and admiration from others.

8. Both codependent people, and sociopaths/psychopaths/narcissists, have an unhealthy relationship with themselves. One puts others before themselves, while the other puts themselves over others. Both interlock as abuser and victim, just like two pieces of a puzzle.

9. Codependency can also exist between a parent and a child.

10. A codependent parent holds their child responsible for the parent's unhappiness and expects the child to compensate by complying with all their demands.

11. The codependent parent thinks they are always right and tries to impose their views on the child. They use crying, yelling, or silent treatment to gain the advantage in any arguments.

12. Codependent parents are poor listeners and never listen to, or consider, their child's feelings and opinions. They also exhibit rapid mood swings to avoid responsibility and guilt.

13. Codependent parents always wish to control their child, and use subtle manipulation to achieve the same.

14. In mild cases of codependent parents, you should set your boundaries, impose them firmly, and look for a family therapist to help overcome the issue.

15. If the problem is insoluble, it's best to end the relationship with codependent parents.

In the next chapter, you will learn....

- How to avoid emotional blackmail.
- How to defeat emotional blackmail.
- Non-defensive communication skills to stop emotional blackmail.
- Developing boundaries and mental resilience.

CHAPTER SEVEN:

Dealing With Emotional Blackmail

Emotional blackmail is not a pleasant experience, but unfortunately, many of us succumb to it at various stages of our lives. The truth is there are many people out there ready to prey upon you and exploit you for their advantage. It's crucial you know about emotional blackmail, the tactics used, and where you can find these parasitic personalities.

After discussing all this, we come to the most interesting and significant part. That is how to deal with emotional blackmail.

Here's the ultimate guide to deal with emotional blackmail:

Recognize the red flag situations

Red flag situations are absolutely, without any doubt, pointing towards emotional blackmail. Being aware of these situations is the first step to deal with the threat and make it powerless.

Ask yourself if you find yourself apologizing for your actions even though you weren't wrong or at fault? Observe if your partner is ever prepared to take 'No' for an answer. Do you always find yourself giving in to your spouse or partner's wishes at the expense of your own? Perhaps you may have noticed that you always seem to be the one who makes the sacrifices and compromises in the relationship. Worst of all, does your spouse or partner intimidate or threaten you into complying with their demands?

Know the typical emotional blackmail tactic

People who employ these tactics use Fear>Obligation>Guilt as their favorite way of getting what they want.

At first, the blackmailer tries to make the victim fearful, angry, or disappointed. This makes the target feel obligated to meet the demands. If the victim still doesn't comply, the manipulator instills feelings of guilt in them for not abiding by the abuser's wishes.

All this is done in a very subtle manner to appeal to the victim's sensibilities. They play manipulation in a way that the victim thinks their demands are reasonable, and they should agree to them.

If you feel yourself to be the victim of this FOG technique, ask a close friend or a relative to give you a different perspective on the relationship, and tell you what they see or feel from the outside.

Know if you are vulnerable

People who have trouble saying 'No' are most susceptible to emotional blackmail. If you are one of them, allow yourself to get comfortable with the idea of refusing. Think of the tone and the words you'll use to signify empowerment and say 'No' to other's manipulation in future.

How to stop emotional blackmail?

1. There are times when you need to give priority to your wants, needs, and preferences over those of your partner.
2. Stand up for your truth, views, and opinions, and become more assertive and self-protective.

3. Set clear boundaries of what you'll accept and what you won't. Boundaries shouldn't be overstepped in any circumstances.

4. Realizing your well-being comes first even if you love your partner dearly. Share your personal priorities and make compromises accordingly.

5. Don't give in to the emotional blackmail; it will make the situation worse.

6. If your loved one threatens you with physical violence, immediately leave the situation and alert the relevant authorities.

7. Reach out to your close friends or social support system and seek professional help from a therapist if necessary.

Are you emotionally blackmailing someone?

Besides being the victim, you can also be an offender. None of us are immune to that tendency. Observe your patterns in getting others to do what you'd like. What is your response when someone argues with you or doesn't do what you'd like? Do you implore? Get punitive? Punish through not providing love and affection? Do you take their opposition as a threat to the relationship? Do you respond with remarks like "If you loved me, you would have done so and so"?

If you answer in the affirmative to any of these, you may well be blackmailing others, either knowingly or unknowingly. So you must admit and acknowledge this. This is a way of taking responsibility for your actions and creates a climate of safety and repair for yourself and the other person.

Tell the person you have been manipulating that you are aware of your actions. Saying sorry won't be enough, though. You have to assure the person that you are ready to own your actions and seek to change the way you behave. Ask the person you have hurt what they need from you to feel they can trust you. Find ways to resolve the issues together and move forward.

How to defeat emotional blackmail?

First, read the following checklist to know if you are a victim of emotional blackmail:

- You tell yourself that giving in is OK.
- You believe that giving in is fine to calm the other person down.
- You feel that what you want is incorrect.
- You think it's better to give in now; you'll oppose it another time.
- You feel that it is better to surrender than to offend someone.
- You don't usually make a stand.
- You give away your power.
- You do what other people want, not what you want.
- You accept everything without protest.
- You give up things you like to placate the other person.

If any of these strike a chord with you, you could well be the victim of emotional blackmail. So, now it's time to gather your courage and make changes in yourself. Grab that personal maturity and take the position that will stop you being a victim; take a stand for yourself.

Take a moment to look at your past and see if that complacency is automatic, inherited, or the result of some acquired habit in childhood. It can be difficult and daunting to shift your perspective from being a victim and change the dynamics, but it's well worth it. Reach out for support when needed.

When you are emotionally blackmailed in a relationship, you still have choices. You can let things stay as they are, or work towards a healthier situation, or decide the relationship will have to end. There are tactics, abilities, and life-style changes to alter the situation before you decide to give in or give up.

You need two things to defeat the person who blackmails you emotionally:

- Learn and develop the skills of non-defensive communication.
- Develop your boundaries and mental resilience.

When you decide to shift yourself out of a situation of emotional blackmail, it requires a lot of courage and willpower to tolerate the feeling of displeasing your loved ones. Sometimes, that can bring up past anxieties. Many of our fears are derived from past experiences, even though we mistake them as originating from current events. We mix up our earlier lives with the present, and therefore, when we get hurt, we act according to our past experience. We can and will do anything to protect ourselves from anxieties over other people's reactions.

But, if you separate the present from your past, you'll have more confidence and many more choices for how you respond. Don't see yourself as weak or incapable. Your personal history need not continue to dictate your present. Believe in yourself, and have the strength and resilience to handle change. Despite feeling fearful, allow yourself to go with it.

Along with fear, comes guilt which can be a major contributor to your problems. Just as you allow yourself to cope with fear, you can tolerate this guilt too! Your dignity, self-respect, and emotional health will ultimately thank you for doing so.

Take a closer look at your fears and guilt. Ask yourself the following questions:

- Am I doing anything spiteful?
- Am I being cruel?
- Did I do anything abusive?
- Did I insult someone or wanted to insult them?
- Is what I did humiliating someone?
- Is my behavior insulting?
- Am I being harmful by doing this?

If your answer is an honest 'No' to these questions, then there's nothing you should be guilty of. If it's 'Yes,' then you need to change the way you behave. Changing might seem uncomfortable in the beginning, but try to see this discomfort as a new start in your relationship, as a way to greater maturity.

Many people think that they need to become stronger before they can take constructive steps towards defeating emotional blackmail. The truth is that as you start shifting to a new set of thought and conduct, the sense of your strength will ensue automatically.

Others may feel surprised by your alteration and may react adversely. Allow for this; don't take it personally. Don't back out from changing your determination not to accept emotional blackmail. It won't feel terrific at first, but that's still all right.

The tactics of an abuser thrive on confrontation and escalation. The victim is pushed lower and lower in the power structure. When we are emotionally connected to someone and receive criticism from them, we naturally tend to get defensive. However, defensiveness creates a similar response in the other person. Find non-defensive ways to communicate with your blackmailer, they won't be able to get to you, and you can shift the dynamic.

Remember this mantra! Next time when anybody asks you to do something you are not happy with, the first thing to do is STOP. Take a deep breath. This helps you pull out of the situation and any habitual ways you might have of reacting defensively.

Instead of a blunt 'Yes' or 'No,' say, "I am unable to take the decision just at the moment; I need to think about this." That will allow you time to calm down, gather your strength, and connect with your thoughts without anxiety and pressure. When you are in balance and can double-check with both your intellect and emotions, you can make a healthy decision.

How to develop the skills of non-defensive communication?

Non-defensive communication is a style of communication that avoids the defensive maneuvers and power struggles that tend to fuel an argument or conflict.

The opposite of non-defensive communication is the 'war model,' which increases the conflict because the focus is on winning the argument rather than solving the problem. Communication under the 'war model' elicits a defensive response that activates the emotional part of your brain that controls the 'fight or flight' response. As a result, the person reacts impulsively and not rationally. This reduces their capacity to communicate effectively.

When we're defensive, we engage in power struggles as a part of the 'flight or fight' response. Sometimes, the person even withdraws and surrenders. This vulnerability makes one susceptible to hurt or attack.

We all have a natural tendency to get defensive to protect ourselves from criticism. When you get defensive while communicating with others, you make it harder for people around you to listen to what you say. It also gets difficult to hear their side of things.

You might have observed this during critical conversations with your spouse, boss, co-worker, or friend. When you get defensive, the other person is likely to respond the same way. The result is ultimately frustration and exhaustion, where neither of you gets what you want.

To avoid this happening, develop your non-defensive communication skills by following these three steps:

1. State your observation

To start your conversation in a non-defensive way, avoid blaming the other person for the problem. Be careful not to make character assassinations about the opposite person. Instead, focus on what you see or hear.

For example, instead of saying, "You didn't iron the clothes," say, "I see the clothes are not ironed."

Or instead of "You are always late," say, "I seem to be the first one to arrive at the office."

When you use "I" statements, you sound less critical and make your listener feel less defensive when compared to the statements starting with "You."

2. Describe your feelings

Follow-up your observation with a comment regarding how that behavior made you feel. This helps the listener relate better to the problem in question. Expressing your feelings here is more than a one-word answer to, "How do you feel about a particular thing?" You must identify your feelings properly and narrate them in detail to relate more effectively to the person you are talking to.

For example, in place of, "You make me angry," say, "I am feeling frustrated and stuck."

3. Request a specific behavior

The most critical part of non-defensive conversation is how to make requests for different attitudes and actions in the future. By making such a request, you let the other person know you aren't holding any grudges or complaints against them. Instead, you wish to work towards a constructive solution to the problem.

For example, "I would appreciate it if you could move those papers off the dining table before dinner."

If you follow the above steps diligently, you can quickly learn the skills of non-defensive communication, and make your conversations successful. By being polite and respectful in communicating, you play the role of a 'bigger person.'

Don't bottle things up. Don't wait to bring up the issue; otherwise, your suppressed emotions will escalate, and you won't be able to keep your conversation productive.

Non-defensive communication takes practice and time to bear fruit. Hang in there with it; it's worth the effort.

Non-defensive communication requires a person to change their core attitude. It obliges them to alter the way in which they ask questions, give feedback, express feelings, and offer opinions. They may well have to change their tone of voice, phrasing, and body language.

Once you follow these steps of non-defensive communication with persistence, you feel empowered. The blackmailer can't successfully attack you or rob you of your powers.

How to stand up for yourself at the workplace without being defensive

In the workplace, not everyone plays fair office politics. You'll find people talking about your work in a way that can negatively impact your reputation. A person may falsely accuse you of something wrong or take credit for your work. Misunderstanding can ensue with people pointing fingers at you.

It's critical you stand up for yourself. You can't afford to stay quiet waiting for the 'truth' to come out by itself. You have to play an active role in standing up for yourself to build or defend your reputation.

Besides standing up for yourself, it's important how you do it. Standing up for yourself is a communication skill that needs practice and time to master. You have to do it without sounding hostile. If you use an aggressive mode of communication, it'll be tough to get people to listen to your side of the story.

Let's say something happened at your workplace. You'll have your perception of what happened, and others will have their view of what happened. The two may not coincide. When you try to forcefully convince others of your perception, you are basically attacking them. You'll be using the classic, "He said, she said" phrases, and you'll sound defensive. The more you insist you're the one telling the truth, the more it implies that the other person is lying. You'll only sound worse. The goal of standing up for yourself is to maintain your poise, show others that you're confident of your work, and they can't easily take advantage of you.

Follow these 4 tips to stand up for yourself without sounding blunt and defensive:

1. Stay cool and use a calm tone

That's hard to do when someone has said bad things about you, but it's crucial if you want to take the best approach to stand up for yourself. Your communication becomes sharp and vengeful when your emotions dominate your judgment. When you act through your emotions, you'll sound defensive and vulnerable without achieving the goal of standing up for yourself in the best way. On the other hand, if you are composed, people are more likely to listen to what you say.

2. Communicate your perspective without blaming others

When someone accuses you of doing something wrong, it's an impulsive reaction to say, "No, I didn't do it. They are lying." Such a statement tends to sound defensive. Alternatively, you can say something like, "I am surprised by this news. I am not sure why you perceived that I did this, but I respectfully disagree." Taking this path, you focus your conversation on your reactions, and the facts pointing towards you, instead of the person who accused you.

3. Be the bigger person

Sometimes people misunderstand what happens, and this leads to miscommunication. They point the gun at you because they fail to understand the situation from your point of view. Instead of pointing fingers at them, be the bigger person, and respond by saying, "This is perhaps a misunderstanding." This way, you'll appear more generous and willing to build healthy relationships at the workplace.

4. Support your perspective with facts

You can't present your case without any facts to prove it. Don't alter them to turn the situation in your favor. Just present the facts that support why you disagree with others without blaming them. It's also important to know when to stand up for yourself. When in a group setting, if someone says you did something which you didn't do, it's not always advisable to make a forceful stand then and there. You can simply say that you are surprised by their accusations, and you disagree. Remember, it could be a misunderstanding. In that instance, you still stood up for yourself in front of the group, but did so without blaming the person and going into details. It shows your poise and communication skills, which will leave a good impression.

How to develop mental resilience?

Life is hard sometimes. When adversity strikes, can you recover quickly? Do you adapt? Or do you feel as though you have no choice other than to go under? If so, that suggests you don't naturally have a great deal of resilience. However, it's not a thing to worry about. There are many ways you can improve your mental resilience. You can learn and hone it through practice, hard work, and discipline.

Our lives can be challenged by different circumstances. That might be a bereavement, losing our job, or the end of a relationship. Despite this, such challenges provide an opportunity to develop into a stronger person.

How to be mentally strong?

Mental strength means being able to cope with stressful situations, problems, and challenges in our lives. It's the occasions when we rise to the challenge, and do our best, even if we're in difficult situations. Building mental strength is fundamental to leading our best life. Just as we exercise and eat the right foods for our physical health, we must also develop our mental muscles by using psychological tools and techniques.

Good mental health helps us have happier lives, have better friendships and social ties, and does wonders for our confidence. It helps us to deal with the difficult situations we may find ourselves in.

In order to have stable mental health, you must work at it. It can take a while to see results, but it can be done. Just as you see physical gains by regular exercise, mental strength is built by developing good psychological methods that enhance our minds and spirits.

For physical health, you must leave behind things like junk food. Similarly, for mental gain, you should get rid of unhealthy habits like self-pity or blaming others.

Building resilience and mental toughness

The American Psychological Association defines Mental Resilience as *"The process of adapting well in the face of adversity, trauma, tragedy, threats, or even significant sources of stress."*

On the same lines, Mental Toughness is the ability to stay strong in the face of adversity, to keep your focus and determination, despite the difficulties you face. A mentally tough individual sees adversity and challenges as an opportunity rather than a threat, and has confidence and a positive approach to deal with them constructively.

The 4 C's of mental toughness

1. Control

Are you in control of your life, including your emotions and sense of purpose? The extent to which you are in control of these elements indicates your level of mental toughness. This control component can be considered as your self-esteem.

The higher you are on the Control scale, the more comfortable you are in yourself. You can control your emotions well, be less likely to reveal your emotional state to others, and you'll be less distracted by other people's attitudes and feelings.

Being lower on the Control scale means you take situations personally and believe you can do nothing about what has taken place.

2. Commitment

This is the measure of your personal focus and reliability. If you are High on the commitment scale, you can effectively set goals and achieve them consistently without getting distracted. You are good at establishing practices and strategies that cultivate success.

On the other hand, being Low on the commitment scale indicates your difficulty in setting and prioritizing your goals or adapting habits indicative of success. You also get easily distracted by other people or competing priorities.

The Control and Commitment scales represent the Resilience part of mental toughness. The ability to respond positively to setbacks requires a sense of knowing that you are in control of your life and can make a change. You also need focus and an ability to establish habits and targets that will get you back on track to achieve your goals.

3. Challenge

Challenge is the extent to which you are motivated and can adapt. Being high on the Challenge scale means you are determined to achieve your personal best and see adversity as an opportunity instead of a threat. You are psychologically agile and flexible. Being Low on the Challenge scale means you see change as a threat and avoid difficult situations for fear of failure.

4. Confidence

Confidence is your ability to be productive and capable. It's your belief in yourself that you can influence others. Being high on the Confidence scale means you believe that you will successfully complete tasks, take setbacks in your stride while maintaining and strengthening your resolve. Being Low on the Confidence scale shows that you easily get upset by disappointments, and believe that you aren't capable, or that you lack ability to influence other people.

The Challenge and Confidence scales represent the Confidence part of Mental Toughness. They represent a person's ability to identify and seize an opportunity and see the situations as opportunities to explore. If you are confident in yourself, you can easily interact with others and are likely to convert problems into successful outcomes.

How to Build Resilience?

Resilience can be improved through concentration, good habits, and hard work. There are many strategies for the same. However, you need to identify the way that works best for you. Your level of mental resilience is not something that is decided upon by random factors. It can be improved throughout your life.

So here are the different strategies and techniques to improve your mental resilience:

1. Developing new skills

Learning new skills is an integral part of building resilience because it helps to build confidence in your ability to learn and grow. These inner and outer qualities can be utilized during challenging times, and also increase your self-esteem and ability to solve problems. You can invest in learning new activities through competency-based learning.

Also, if you can acquire new skills in a group setting, there's nothing like that. It gives you an added advantage of social support, which also helps in building resilience.

2. Setting your goals

Develop the ability to set out what you want to achieve, measuring out the steps by which you will get there, and acting accordingly. This will help to develop will-power and mental resilience. These goals can be anything related to your physical health, emotional well being, career, finance, or spirituality.

If you have goals that require you to learn new skills, it will have a double benefit, perhaps something like learning a new language or learning to play an instrument. Setting and working towards goals that have a spiritual dimension, doing voluntary work for disadvantaged people, can be immensely rewarding and helps in building resilience. This is because such activities provide a more profound insight into life, which is valuable during tough times.

3. Controlled Exposure

Controlled or gradual exposure to anxiety-provoking situations helps people overcome their fears much more quickly. Research studies show that this can build resilience, along with skill-acquisition and goal-setting strategies.

For example, public speaking is a useful life skill, but it also tends to create anxiety in many people. Such individuals could set goals of controlled exposure to acquire the ability to do this. They could begin by speaking in public to a small number of friends. Then, having gained some confidence in doing that, they can then move on to larger audiences.

The American Psychology Association further shares 11 strategies for building mental resilience:

1. Make connections

You can strengthen your resilience through healthy links to family, friends, and community. Building relationships with people in your life who are important to you, and who will help you when times are hard, all these things can be immensely useful in lifting our spirits and encouraging us to feel there is light at the end of the tunnel. Similarly, when you help others in their tough times, it helps you as well.

2. Crises are not Disasters

Even though problems may confront us, it's vital to bear in mind that our reactions are what makes us. If we deal with what is in front of us and look to the future, we can have confidence that things will change for the better. This simple faith can make us feel better and give us the necessary power to deal with the situation.

3. Accept that change is inevitable

Life is, by its nature, prone to constant change. What we might want at one period of our life may have altered a few years down the road. It may be that some objectives may have to be changed. By accepting the factors you can't change, or which are not under your control, it allows you to focus on those subjects that can realistically be dealt with.

4. Move towards your goals

Besides setting your goals, it's also important to make sure they are realistic. Creating small, actionable steps makes your goals attainable. Try for practical realistic accomplishments on the way to achieving the major prize. Try to accomplish things in small increments instead of trying to do everything all at once.

5. Take decisive actions

Instead of running away from problems, or daydreaming that they will go away, resolve to take decisive action to solve them in the best way possible.

6. Look for self-discovery opportunities

Misfortunes in your life create stress but can be a meaningful source of learning and personal growth. Finding out how to cope with a difficult situation, and successfully coming through it, can boost your confidence, improve your spirits, strengthen your relationships, and teach you deeper truths. You can unlock your hidden strengths during these challenging times. Sometimes, it can be a journey that makes us appreciate life all the more.

7. Think positively about yourself

Working towards your goals and improving your confidence helps in preventing difficulties and building resilience. Having a positive view of yourself is also at the core of problem-solving.

8. Keep things in perspective

When things get tough, remember that many people experience similar hardships in their lives. It is, in the end, all part of being human. Don't let yourself see the problem as worse than it is. Make sure you keep one eye on the future when times seem challenging in the present.

9. Maintain a hopeful outlook

When you focus on the negative part of the situation, you can give way to your fears and find it hard to know what to do. Keep your spirits up, and be confident you can solve the difficulty. Work out how you can cope with it, and you will probably surprise yourself.

10. Take care of yourself

Looking after yourself is something that shouldn't be underestimated. It will help you to deal all the better with hard and stressful circumstances. Self-care should include things like paying attention to your feelings, and doing things that help you to feel happier and more content. Taking up hobbies, exercising, engaging in creative pursuits are all extremely useful.

11. Other ways to strengthen resilience

It can be a great idea to undertake a course in meditation or similar mental disciplines. Techniques such as this are certainly of immense help in calming your mind and thereby improving your resilience.

Strategies for building resilience

As said before, the right approach to building resilience will vary between different people. Every individual reacts in their own way to traumatic and stressful life events. Therefore, what might work for one person may not work for another.

Here are some common strategies to employ for building resilience:

Learn from your past

Take a look at your past experiences and sources of personal strength to get insight as to which resilience-building strategies will work for you. The American Psychology Association recommends asking these questions to yourself to judge how you've reacted to challenging situations in the past:

1. What types of events have been most stressful for you?
2. How have those events affected you?
3. Did it help to think of important people in your life when distressed?
4. Who did you go to for support when working through a trauma?
5. What have you learned about yourself during challenging times?
6. Is it helpful for you to assist someone else with a similar experience?
7. Have you been able to overcome obstacles, and if so, how?
8. What makes you feel more hopeful about the future?

Be flexible

Being resilient means having a flexible mindset. When undergoing stressful circumstances and events in your life, it is necessary to maintain flexibility and balance in the following ways:

1. Allow yourself to experience strong emotions, and realize when you have to push them aside to continue functioning.
2. Take the necessary action to deal with your problems and meet the demands of daily living, but also know when to step back and rest/re-energize yourself.
3. Spend time with your loved ones who offer support and encouragement; nurture yourself.
4. Rely on others, but also know when to rely on yourself.

Sometimes, the support of family and friends is not enough. Know when to seek assistance from outside, such as self-help and community support groups, books and publications, online resources, or a licensed mental health professional.

Books, publications, and online resources offer a wealth of information where you can hear/read how others have successfully navigated through tough and challenging situations like yours. These are valuable resources of motivation, inspiration, and ways to deal with stress and trauma. However, make sure you always refer to a reliable source.

Sharing your experiences, emotions, and ideas within support groups can provide relaxation and comfort to you. It will make you feel there's someone to rely on during difficult times.

If other methods prove unsuccessful, it's best to seek professional help from a mental health professional. Talk to a licensed therapist if you can't function in your daily life because of painful life events.

Resilient Relationships

Resilience is also an essential aspect of your relationships. Relationships demand ongoing attention and cultivation, especially during times of adversity.

Certain relationships can survive better than others. That's because they foster resilience in each other.

Seven characteristics of highly resilient relationships

1. **Active optimism**

Optimism is not just hoping that things will get better; instead, it's believing that they will and then taking action. Optimism in a relationship means an agreement to avoid critical, hurtful, and cynical comments, and work together to harness the power of living positively.

2. **Honesty, integrity, accepting responsibility for one's actions, and the willingness to forgive**

When two people involved in a relationship are committed to recognizing the responsibility of their actions, are loyal to each other, and forgive each other, they are likely to cultivate resilience in their relationship.

3. Decisiveness

Having the courage to take action, even when it can provoke anxiety in a relationship is crucial. Decisive action could involve leaving a toxic relationship. Such decisiveness can promote your resilience.

4. Tenacity

Tenacity is perseverance and ability to hold on in the face of discouragement, setbacks, and failures. Remember, there will always be ebbs and flows, good times as well as hard times, in your relationships. But, how much you can hold on is a testament to your tenacity.

5. Self-Control

In the context of relationships, self-control is the ability to control impulses, resist temptations, and delay gratification. These are desirable qualities that help one to avoid negative practices and promote healthy practices, particularly in times of adversity.

6. Honest communication

Open, honest communication maintains the sense of 'belonging' and connectedness in a relationship. Sometimes, the most difficult conversations are the most important ones to have.

7. Presence of Mind

Presence of mind has many positive implications for you as well as your partner. This awareness leads to calm, non-judgemental thinking, and open communication between the couple. It also enables collaborative thinking and openness to new solutions, rather than blaming and condemning each other.

How to become resilient for life?

If you wish to have strong mental resilience for the rest of your life, start building it right now! Practice the strategies and tips discussed above with perseverance; over time, you will increase your ability to bounce back and adapt to your hardships.

The craziest thing about experiencing adverse events is that the more you flex your resilience muscle, the better you'll be able to respond next time.

Developing your emotional boundaries in relationships

The second way to beat emotional blackmail is to set your boundaries. The most important question that may click in your mind right now is, "Why should I have boundaries? How can setting boundaries save me from emotional blackmail?"

Setting healthy personal boundaries fosters healthy relationships, increases your self-esteem, and reduces stress, anxiety, and frustration. Boundaries help protect you by clearly defining what you accept and what you don't in any relationship.

Boundaries include physical as well as emotional boundaries. Physical boundaries include your body, personal space, and privacy. If anybody stands too close to you, touches you inappropriately, or flips through the files on your phone, they violate your physical boundaries.

Emotional boundaries include separating your feelings from that of others. Taking responsibility for another's feelings, letting them dictate your feelings, sacrificing your needs to please others, blaming others for your problems, and taking excessive responsibility for their difficulties are violations of your emotional boundaries.

When you have strong boundaries, they protect your self-esteem and your identity as an individual, and your right to make choices in life.

Setting boundaries is not sufficient unless you protect them too. But, most of us find it difficult to set healthy boundaries consistently, especially the emotional ones. It's tricky sometimes to even identify when these boundaries get crossed. The reason is the fear of consequences to our relationships by setting them.

The red flags of violation to your boundaries are - discomfort, stress, anxiety, resentment, fear, and guilt. These feelings occur from the sense of being taken advantage of or not being appreciated.

Ask yourself if the following statements resonate with you:

- You can't make your own decisions.
- You can't ask for what you need.
- You can't say No.
- You feel criticized.
- You feel responsible for other people's feelings.
- You seem to take on their moods.
- You often feel nervous, anxious, and worried around those people.

If you have vague boundaries, or none at all, you'll have a weak sense of self-identity, and a feeling of disempowerment in making the decisions of your life. In consequence, you'll rely on your partner for your happiness and decision-making responsibility, thereby losing important parts of your identity; this creates the risk of becoming codependent.

The inability to set boundaries also results from the fear of abandonment in a relationship, fear of being judged, and fear of hurting someone else's feelings.

The first step to building better boundaries is to know what your limits are. Who you are, what you're responsible for, and what you aren't responsible for. You are responsible for your happiness, your behavior, your choices, and feelings. You cannot be held to account for someone else's happiness, behavior, choices, and feelings.

Emotional boundaries and boundary traps

Emotional boundaries fall into the categories of time, energy, emotions, and values. However, beware of the boundary traps in a relationship. Do you recognize any of the following thoughts, or things you may have said?

- I don't have my own identity. My identity comes from my partner, and I'll do anything and everything to make them happy.
- This relationship is better than my last one.
- I spend all my time fulfilling my partner's goals and activities. I have no time to do what I want to do.
- My partner will be lost if I am not there.
- This relationship will get better if I give more time to it.
- Most of the time, the relationship is great, except for a few occasions, and that's enough for me.

How to set your emotional boundaries?

First, commit to yourself to put your identity, needs, feelings, and goals on priority. Healthy emotional boundaries start with a belief and acceptance of how you are at present. Let go of the responsibility to fix others, to be responsible for the outcome of someone else's choices, saving or rescuing others, depending on their approval, and changing yourself to be liked by others.

Prepare a list of boundaries you want to strengthen. Don't just jot them down, but visualize yourself setting them, and assertively communicating them to others. Boundary setting is a process. So start small by setting non-threatening boundaries first, experience success with them, and then move on to more challenging ones.

Here are a few to start with:

- Say no to the tasks you don't want to do or don't have time to do.
- Be ready to help.
- Thank others without apology, regret, or shame.
- Ask for help when required.
- Delegate tasks to your partner or family members.
- Don't overcommit to anything. Protect your time.
- Ask for your personal space.
- Speak out when faced with behavior that infringes on your space.
- Honor yourself and your needs.
- Drop the guilt and responsibility for others.
- Share personal information gradually and in a mutual way.

When you are setting your boundaries and shifting the dynamic in the relationship, you are likely to encounter resistance from the other person. Stick to your guns, and keep on communicating your needs. The 'broken record technique' comes in handy at this moment. Repeat the statement as many times as needed.

Healthy relationships are a balance of give and take. You feel calm, safe, supported, respected, cared for, and unconditionally accepted in a healthy relationship. You are free to be who you are and encouraged to be the best version of yourself.

Similarly, healthy boundaries are also a sign of emotional health, self-respect, and strength. By setting your boundaries, you set high standards for those around you. Expect to be treated the same way you treat them. You'll soon find yourself surrounded by people who respect you, care for you, your feelings, needs, and treat you with kindness.

Chapter Summary

1. To deal with emotional blackmail, you first need to identify the red flag situations of the tactic.
2. If you always apologize to your partner, even for the right actions, if you can't say No to your partner, if you always make sacrifices, or give in to your partner's demands at the expense of your own, you are the victim of emotional blackmail.
3. Know the typical FOG technique or the tactics of Fear, Obligation, and Guilt used by blackmailers to manipulate you.
4. If you find it difficult to say No to your partner or in any relationship, you are vulnerable to emotional blackmail. Get comfortable in refusing the demands that don't align with your best interests.
5. Give priority to your needs, stand up for your truth, views, and opinions to stop emotional blackmail.
6. Set clear boundaries of what behavior you'll accept and what you won't. Make sure your boundaries can't be overstepped under any circumstances.
7. Observe your actions to know if you aren't employing any of those tactics to manipulate others. If yes, admit and acknowledge your manipulative behavior, say sorry about it, and assure your target that you're ready to change your ways. Make them feel the trust and safety in your relationship.
8. You need two things to defeat emotional blackmail - developing the skills of non-defensive communication, and developing your emotional boundaries and mental resilience.
9. Non-defensive communication is the best way to deal with a blackmailer. It is a way of expressing your thoughts and feelings to others without getting defensive or pointing fingers at others.
10. When you use a defensive mode of communication, the other person also gets defensive in turn. This makes it difficult for them to hear your side of the story.

11. You can communicate in a non-defensive way by stating your observation about the situation, describing your feelings by using "I" statements and requesting different behavior in future.

12. Your mental strength is your capacity to deal effectively with stressful situations and perform to the best of your ability.

13. Mental strength can be developed over time by choosing the habits of personal development.

14. Mental resilience is the process of adapting well to the adversities in your life.

15. Mental toughness is the ability to stay strong in the face of adversity and keep your focus and determination.

16. Control over your emotions, commitment towards your goals, ability to be productive, capable, and adapting to the adversities of life are central aspects of mental toughness.

17. Your mental resilience level is not decided upon at birth; you can develop it through will power, discipline, and hard work.

18. There are different strategies and techniques to build your mental resilience. Choose the one that works best for you.

19. Resilience is also important for healthy relationships. Relationships that foster resilience in each other have better chances of survival than others.

FINAL WORDS

A healthy relationship helps you evolve into a better version of yourself. It enables you to grow into a kind and confident personality.

If you feel suffocated and controlled in a relationship; if your needs don't matter, or you feel unsafe to express your thoughts and feelings with that person, your relationship has transformed into a toxic one.

Toxicity can creep into the dearest and closest relationships. It could be between parent and child, your spouse, lover, or a close friend. Toxicity invades a relationship when one person starts manipulating the other to give in to their demands without recognizing or respecting the other's needs.

Manipulation may sometimes seem harmless, but is actually an emotional blackmail, an emotional abuse. That's because the emotional blackmailer uses your feelings negatively against you to get what they want. In short, they control you and your behavior in order to fulfill their demands.

It's essential to be aware of the signs of emotional blackmail. Develop awareness that you are being manipulated. Otherwise, the person will continue to blackmail you, and you'll end up with frustration, anxiety, and low self-esteem. If you aren't aware of the signs of emotional blackmail, you can't deal with it or stop it.

Here are some examples of manipulation used by an emotional blackmailer:

- Threats to endanger your life.
- Threats that they will kill themself if you don't obey their wishes.

- Control you by using money.
- Threats to end the relationship with you.
- Manipulate you into feeling compassionate for him/her.
- Making you feel guilty.
- Demoralizing you.
- Hurting you emotionally.
- Depriving you of love, care, and appreciation.
- Making you feel selfish and inconsiderate.

The blackmailer uses clever and covert techniques to make you believe that his/her demands are reasonable, and you must comply with them. However, the more you concede, the worse the situation gets.

Moreover, the emotional blackmailer gets to know your fears, the deep-rooted ones like fear of failure, isolation, and humiliation, which they use against you to get their demands fulfilled.

But why do some people resort to emotional blackmail?

Emotional blackmail is usually used as a weapon to gain control over someone else's thoughts and feelings. Such people are generally emotionally insecure, possibly due to their experience of similar abuse in childhood. As a result, they can't differentiate what is right and what is wrong.

Since they grew up being emotionally manipulated themselves, they believe it to be the right way of asking for things or obtaining their demands. They mistakenly believe that by making others feel powerless and vulnerable, they'll feel powerful and good about themselves.

Every person who resorts to emotional blackmail suffers from low self-esteem, lack of empathy, and a tendency to blame others for the problems in their lives.

However, it's important to note that it's not '*the wants*' that qualify for labeling the person as an emotional blackmailer, rather how he/she goes about fulfilling those '*wants.*' If he/she threatens you or gets insensitive to your needs, the term 'emotional blackmailer' is justified for them.

Indeed, there are 6 progressive stages of emotional blackmail:

1. In the first stage, the blackmailer tells you about his/her demands and adds an emotional threat.
2. Second, you resist the demand of the blackmailer.
3. Since the blackmailer can't tolerate any refusal, they put pressure on you to comply.
4. They repeat their threat as a consequence of your denial.
5. Affected by negative emotions, you decide to give in to the blackmailer's demands.
6. As a result, a pattern is set where the blackmailer knows your hot buttons and how to push them to get what they want.

The pressure they build upon you for compliance is basically through three tactics - Fear, Obligation, and Guilt, commonly known as the FOG technique.

Most of us have different kinds of fears like fear of isolation, fear of the unknown, apprehension about confrontation, worry about abandonment, fear of tricky situations, etc. Emotional blackmailers know your weak points, and how they can use them to get what they want.

Using your sense of obligation to press your emotional triggers and manipulate you is yet another favorite technique of emotional blackmailers. They can make you feel guilty for not keeping up your promises as per your obligations.

All these tactics stem from cowardice. Emotional blackmailers can't tolerate failure, loss, deprivation, and frustration. The moment they experience these feelings, they spring into action and resort to emotional blackmail to get what they want and remove these negative feelings.

You can classify emotional blackmailers into 4 categories:

1. **Punishers** who threaten to punish you physically, with financial penalties, or ending the relationship with you if you don't do what they want.
2. **Self-punishers** who threaten to harm themselves if you don't comply with their wishes.
3. **Sufferers** who blame you for their low emotional state, and expect you to do what they want to make them feel better.
4. **Tantalizers** who lure you with a false promise of something better if you do what they desire.

Whatever the tactics they use, if you find yourself apologizing for things you aren't doing, or find you're the only one making sacrifices in a relationship, or the other person insists on only their way, or you feel you're being threatened into obeying their demands - you are the victim of emotional blackmail.

However, it takes two to blackmail. Unless you give in to the demands, emotional blackmail can't happen. It may be that your need to please people, fear of their anger, abandonment or conflicts in relationships, extreme compassion and empathy, tendency to take the burden of other's lives on yourself, and low self-esteem make you vulnerable to such individuals.

To change this dynamic and stop being emotionally blackmailed, you must first recognize the red flags of emotional blackmail as detailed in this book. Next, commit to taking care of yourself. Resolve not to let this abusive treatment continue.

Give due respect to your needs first. Detach yourself from the blackmailer's emotions and look at the situation from a different perspective. Don't be tempted to give in to the blackmailer's demands instantly. Pause, take time to evaluate if you should comply or not, and then make your decision.

Use the strategies detailed in this book to develop your mental resilience, and develop the skills of non-defensive communication to talk to the emotional blackmailer.

Finally, set your emotional boundaries and express clearly what you'll accept and what you won't accept. In this way, you can permanently put a stop to emotional blackmail in your life.

SOURCES

Galinsky, L. (2018, November 13). The Use of Emotional Blackmail in a Relationship. Retrieved from https://goodmenproject.com/featured-content/remember-that-time-you-wanted-a-relationship-for-all-the-wrong-reasons-wcz/

Doll, K. (2019, June 19). 18+ Ways to Handle Emotional Blackmail (+ Examples & Quotes). Retrieved from https://positivepsychology.com/emotional-blackmail/

Emotional Blackmail. (n.d.). Retrieved from https://www.merriam-webster.com/dictionary/emotional%20blackmail

Understanding Emotional Blackmail. (2019, January 14). Retrieved from https://claritychi.com/emotional-blackmail/

Hammond, C. (2017, October 10). What is Emotional Blackmail. Retrieved from https://pro.psychcentral.com/exhausted-woman/2016/08/what-is-emotional-blackmail/

Emotional Blackmail Law and Legal Definition. (n.d.). Retrieved from https://definitions.uslegal.com/e/emotional-blackmail/

Paler, J. (2019, December 6). The toxic cycle of emotional blackmail and how to stop it. Retrieved from https://hackspirit.com/emotional-blackmail/

Emotional Blackmail and How it Harms our Kids. (2018, August 1). Retrieved from https://exploringyourmind.com/emotional-blackmail-and-how-it-harms-our-kids/

Johnson, R. S. (2018, August 16). Emotional Blackmail: Fear, Obligation and Guilt . Retrieved from https://www.bpdfamily.com/content/emotional-blackmail-fear-obligation-and-guilt-fog

Go your Own Way. (n.d.). *Emotional Blackmail.* Retrieved from http://www.goyourownway.org/GOYOUROWNWAY/DOCUMENTS/EMOTIONAL%20WELLBEING/EMOTIONAL%20BLACKMAIL.pdf

What Is Emotional Blackmail and 5 Personality Types That Use It. (n.d.). Retrieved from https://www.learning-mind.com/emotional-blackmail/

Four Types Of Emotional Blackmail Manipulators Use Against You. (n.d.). Retrieved from https://www.aconsciousrethink.com/9824/emotional-blackmail/

Kreger, R. (n.d.). Fear, Obligation, and Guilt (FOG) in High Conflict Relationships. Retrieved from https://www.bpdcentral.com/blog/?Fear-Obligation-and-Guilt-FOG-in-High-Conflict-Relationships-36

abcClub. (2018, August 15). Emotional Blackmail_ Feeling like in FOG (fear, obligation, guilt). Retrieved from https://www.youtube.com/watch?v=jPXUQnTSyeU

Mayo Clinic Staff. (n.d.). Borderline personality disorder. Retrieved from
https://www.mayoclinic.org/diseases-conditions/borderline-personality-
disorder/symptoms-causes/syc-20370237

Freedom from the FOG of Emotional Manipulation. (2014, May 23). Retrieved from
https://www.borderline-personality-disorder.com/borderline-personality-disorder-
research/freedom-from-the-fog-of-emotional-manipulation/

Lancer, D. (2019, July 2). Covert Tactics Manipulators Use to Control and Confuse
You. Retrieved from https://www.psychologytoday.com/us/blog/toxic-
relationships/201907/covert-tactics-manipulators-use-control-and-confuse-you

Four Signs of Emotional Blackmail. (n.d.). Retrieved from
https://www.powerofpositivity.com/4-signs-of-emotional-blackmail/

Lancer, Darlene. (n.d.). COMBAT NARCISSISTS' AND ABUSERS' PRIMARY
WEAPON: PROJECTION. Retrieved from
https://www.whatiscodependency.com/narcissist-abuse-empaths-projection/

Murrah, J. D. (n.d.). Breaking the Cycle of Emotional Blackmail. Retrieved from
https://www.streetdirectory.com/travel_guide/7367/parenting/breaking_the_cycle_
of_emotional_blackmail.html

Harley, M. (2017, July 24). What makes a parent toxic? Retrieved from
https://lifelabs.psychologies.co.uk/users/3881-maxine-harley/posts/18860-what-
makes-a-parent-toxic

Avila, T. (2018, November 2). How to Cope with Toxic Parents Whom you Can't
Avoid. Retrieved from https://www.girlboss.com/wellness/toxic-parents

Lancer, D. (2018, August 31). 12 Clues a Relationship with a Parent is Toxic.
Retrieved from https://www.psychologytoday.com/intl/blog/toxic-
relationships/201808/12-clues-relationship-parent-is-toxic

Fellizar, K. (2019, January 23). 7 Seemingly Innocent Things That Can Actually Be
Emotional Blackmail In A Relationship. Retrieved from
https://www.bustle.com/p/7-seemingly-innocent-things-that-can-actually-be-
emotional-blackmail-in-a-relationship-15866011

Centore, A. (2012, November 16). 6 Warning Signs of Emotional Blackmail: Couples
Counseling Tips. Retrieved from https://thriveworks.com/blog/6-warning-signs-
of-emotional-blackmail-couples-counseling-tips/

Griffin, T. (2019, December 4). How to Deal with Emotional Blackmail. Retrieved
from https://www.wikihow.com/Deal-with-Emotional-Blackmail

Steber, C. (2018, April 18). 11 Signs You Are Experiencing Trauma After A Toxic
Relationship. Retrieved from https://www.bustle.com/p/11-signs-you-are-
experiencing-trauma-after-a-toxic-relationship-8759486

Dodd, G. (n.d.). How To Maintain Your Grace After A Bad Breakup. Retrieved from
https://www.bolde.com/how-maintain-grace-after-bad-breakup/

Meurrisse, T. (n.d.). 5 Differences Between Real Love And Attachment. Retrieved
from https://www.lifehack.org/317383/5-differences-between-real-love-and-
attachment

Vaknin, S. (n.d.). Codependence and the Dependent Personality Disorder. Retrieved from https://www.healthyplace.com/personality-disorders/malignant-self-love/codependence-and-the-dependent-personality-disorder

Psychological Manipulation in Treating Codependency. (n.d.). Retrieved from https://emotional-intelligence-training.weebly.com/psychological-manipulation-in-treating-codependency.html

Hunter, D. (2019, March 12). How Codependency Affects Recovery. Retrieved from https://www.rehabcenter.net/how-co-dependency-affects-recovery/

Blackmoor, L. (2016, December 16). 8 Signs You May Have a Codependent Parent. Retrieved from https://wehavekids.com/family-relationships/8-Signs-You-May-Have-a-Codependent-Parent

Dodgson, L. (2018, February 13). 8 warning signs you're in a damaging codependent relationship, according to experts. Retrieved from https://www.businessinsider.in/strategy/8-warning-signs-youre-in-a-damaging-codependent-relationship-according-to-experts/articleshow/62904771.cms

Jewell, T. (2018, January 11). Sociopath: Definition, vs Psychopath, Test, Traits. Retrieved from https://www.healthline.com/health/mental-health/sociopath

Lindeberg, S. (2019, January 9). Psychopath: Meaning, Signs, and vs Sociopath. Retrieved from https://www.healthline.com/health/psychopath

Smith, M. (2019, December 6). Narcissistic Personality Disorder. Retrieved from https://www.helpguide.org/articles/mental-disorders/narcissistic-personality-disorder.htm

Happe, M. (n.d.). The Relationship between Narcissism and Codependency. Retrieved from https://www.mentalhelp.net/blogs/the-relationship-between-narcissism-and-codependency/

Ramirez, J. (n.d.). A Guide To Avoiding and Dealing With Emotional Blackmail. Retrieved from https://www.ba-bamail.com/content.aspx?emailid=19234

Sattin, N. (2016, September 7). Defeating Emotional Blackmail and Manipulation with Susan Forward. Retrieved from https://www.neilsattin.com/blog/2016/09/55-defeating-emotional-blackmail-and-manipulation-with-susan-forward/

Perper, R. (2014, January 29). Non-Defensive Communication In 3 Easy Steps. Retrieved from https://therapychanges.com/blog/2014/01/non-defensive-communication-3-easy-steps/

Israel, L. (2011, September 7). Powerful Non-Defensive Communication: A New Way to Communicate. Retrieved from https://www.maritalmediation.com/2011/09/powerful-non-defensive-communication-a-new-way-to-communicate/

Camins, S. (n.d.). Setting Emotional Boundaries in Relationships. Retrieved from https://roadtogrowthcounseling.com/importance-boundaries-relationships/

Han, L. (n.d.). How to Stand Up for Yourself Without Sounding Defensive. Retrieved from https://bemycareercoach.com/soft-skills/stand-up-for-yourself.html

Ribeiro, M. (2019, December 5). How to Become Mentally Strong: 14 Strategies for Building Resilience. Retrieved from https://positivepsychology.com/mentally-strong/

EXCLUSIVE GIFT

Hello! Thank you for purchasing this book. Here is your free gift. It's good and it's free!

This mini e-book will answer your questions about this rather controversial skill. It's controversial because it works!

Get ready to learn more about Conversational Hypnosis, simplified for easy and practical use.

Here are just a few of the many benefits of learning Conversational Hypnosis:

- Get your audience to warm up to you and be more open to your message
- Better sales tactics
- Create deeper connections with people
- Create positive change
- And more!

If you want to become a good hypnotic conversationalist, you better start learning the skill today and be a master tomorrow. All you have to do is access the secret download page below.

Open a browser window on your computer or smartphone and enter: <u>bonus.emorygreen.com</u>

You will be automatically directed to the download page.

Remember to influence the world with good intentions.

All the best,
Emory Green